RESCUED— NOT MY WILL

BOOK TWO

Shelly Funk
Stephanie Fleming

New Harbor Press

RAPID CITY, SD

Funk & Fleming/New Harbor Press
1601 Mt.Rushmore Rd, Ste 3288
Rapid City, SD 57701
www.newharborpress.com

Rescued - Not My Will, Book II / Shelly Funk & Stephanie Fleming. -- 1st ed.
ISBN 978-1-63357-460-1

CHAPTER ONE

Making the decision on New Year's Eve to take a mission trip to Honduras was a huge step for Jexi. She really wasn't sure what she had signed up for, but everything fell into place seamlessly. Initially, she had been very concerned about how to raise the money for the trip. She should have known that God would open the doors that she needed. They were very close to reaching their goal with the money from the church coffee bar, sales from Aunt Jessie's crafts, her tip money from the diner, and various donations from family and the community. Jexi and Jessie were about seven hundred dollars short and only had a short time to raise the remaining funds. She had asked everyone she could think of and wasn't sure where the rest would come from. But she had learned to trust God and knew in her heart that He would provide.

In the past few weeks, Jexi had been quite busy. She had been working as many hours as she could acquire at the diner and saving practically every penny. She had also been at the church often, sorting donations that people had given them to take to the families in Honduras. She had never felt so needed and alive. What started out as a terrifying thought had become a deep-seated mission in her heart.

She was trying to help Shaya with the initial stages of planning the wedding when she could steal an hour or two away from her other responsibilities. She worried that Shaya would be upset that she did not have a lot of extra time to dedicate to her best friend. But Shaya had assured her that she was fine because she had her family to help. Shaya and Ben had planned a very small and intimate gathering so there weren't many things to do. They had chosen a date in late May, which gave Jexi time to complete her mission trip and return for final preparations.

Time was flying by so quickly. The Monday before they were scheduled to depart, Jexi contacted Shaun to finalize the details of the books he was giving to the students in Honduras. Shaun confirmed that the books were boxed and ready to go.

"Thank you so much, Shaun," Jexi said. "I can't tell you how much this means to us."

"I'm happy to help, Jexi," Shaun replied. "You know I'm a sucker for kids. Especially ones who are in need."

Jexi giggled. "Yeah, I know. These kids are going to flip when they see the books! I'm so excited!"

"By the way," Shaun began, "how are you getting to the airport?"

"Aunt Jessie and I are driving up to KC to stay at Mom and Dad's house overnight. We haven't really talked about getting to the airport, so I guess we can take an Uber or something."

"I'm going to have to get the boxes of books to you somehow," Shaun said. "Why don't I pick you guys up at your folks' place and give you a ride?"

"Oh, you don't have to do that!" Jexi said. "Your donation is enough, really. Jessie and I can come to pick up the boxes."

"Nonsense. Don't waste the extra gas money or money on an Uber. You need every penny you have to save for the trip. Let me help," Shaun countered.

Jexi couldn't disagree. "Okay," she finally consented. "You're right. Thank you."

"Text me the time that you need me to pick you up and I'll be there," Shaun said.

Jexi sighed. "Alright. I will. I can't thank you enough."

"I almost forgot," Shaun quickly added. "We placed a donation jar on the counter at the bookstore. The regulars miss you and have been so willing to help. We have collected two hundred dollars toward your trip!"

Jexi teared up. "Really?" she said with her voice breaking. "I don't know what to say except thank you! I am blown away!"

"It's nothing," Shaun replied.

"It is so much more than that," Jexi answered. "Please tell everyone how grateful I am and that they have been a real blessing."

"Hey, I have an idea," Shaun added. "Why don't you come up a day earlier? We have an event at the bookstore. Maybe you can thank them yourself."

"I love that idea!" Jexi said. "Let me talk to Aunt Jessie and I'll let you know. I'm sure she would be fine with that!"

Jexi hung up the phone with a full heart. She felt like she could almost burst with joy and anticipation. She looked around the apartment to find Shaya. She wanted to share the awesome news. However, Shaya wasn't there. The apartment was quiet. So Jexi looked upward and screamed, "Thank you, God!"

Jexi hurriedly went to her car and drove to the church. She was sure there would be someone there sorting donations. She ran through the front door and immediately encountered Aunt Jessie. The two practically crashed into each other.

"Whoa!" Aunt Jessie exclaimed. "Slow down, hot stuff! Who set your tail on fire?"

"Oh, Aunt Jessie, you'll never guess!" Jexi exclaimed breathlessly. "I just talked to Shaun, my old boss in Kansas City; you remember him, right?" She rushed on without waiting for Jessie to answer. "He is going to help us, and drive us to the airport, and he has collected donations, and the books are ready and I'm so thankful . . . ."

Aunt Jessie put a hand on Jexi's shoulder. "Pause. Take a breath. Now, start over, with a little more space between your words. I didn't catch any of that rambling."

Jexi inhaled deeply. "I just talked to Shaun," she began.

"Good," Aunt Jessie encouraged. "Then what?"

Jexi continued. "He has all the books boxed up and ready to go. He said that he would take the books and us to the airport so we don't have to spend money on an Uber or taxi."

"Well, that's one of the kindest things I've ever heard," said Aunt Jessie.

"And there is more!" Jexi said. "He said that he thinks we should go to KC a day early so I can thank everyone at the bookstore. The employees and customers have collected two hundred dollars for our trip! With those two hundred dollars, we only need five hundred more!"

"By thunder!" Aunt Jessie murmured. She clasped her heart. "God is so good."

"Aunt Jessie?" Jexi inquired. "Are you okay?"

"Oh yes, child," Jessie said. "More than okay! I just never cease to be amazed at the way God works. Come with me into the church office."

Jexi followed her into the office and Jessie pulled out an envelope and handed it to her. "What's that?" Jexi asked.

"Open it and find out," Jessie answered.

Jexi opened the envelope and counted five hundred dollars in cash.

Jexi's eyes opened wide, and she let out a shriek. "Are you kidding?" She flew over to Jessie and gave her a big hug. Then she pulled back and stared at her. "Where . . . how . . . who . . . ?" she began to ask.

"An anonymous donation from the church," Jessie replied.

"Oh, this is truly incredible! We have everything we need," Jexi stated. "You're right, God is so good!" She looked upward once more and whispered, "Thanks again, God!"

Jessie interrupted her thoughts. "Okay, okay, we need to get to sorting. We had more donations come in today."

The two began to walk out of the office when they met the church secretary, Lindy, walking in. Jexi stopped, told Jessie to go on to the gym without her, and that she would be there in a minute.

"Hey, Lindy!" Jexi said. "How are you doing?"

"I'm good!" Lindy replied. "Hey, did you get the mail that I gave to Jessie?"

"Oh yes!" Jexi answered. "We are so excited! It was the final donation that we needed for our trip! I wish I knew who it was so I could thank them, but it was anonymous."

Lindy looked around to see if they were alone. She leaned in close toward Jexi and quietly said, "I know who gave the donation."

Jexi looked at her and waited for a moment. "Really? Can you tell me who it was or are you sworn to secrecy?"

Lindy hesitated. "I'm not really supposed to share that information. You know, church policy and things."

Jexi looked at the floor. "Alright," she said, disheartened.

Lindy saw the disappointment on Jexi's face. "Okay, I'll tell you. But you didn't hear it from me."

Jexi's face perked up. "Thank you!" she said quietly.

Lindy checked the surroundings once more to see if they were still alone. She leaned in a little further and whispered, "Hunter Bennett."

Jexi sucked in a breath. She felt like she had been hit with a two-by-four. "Hunter?" she asked. She composed herself and smiled. "Thanks so much. I won't tell a soul."

She walked away from the office and toward the gym to start helping with the sorting process. She was stunned and pondered why Hunter would give them so much money. *Does Amber know that he did that?* she wondered. *Should I thank him now that I know?* As excited as she was about the mission trip and Shaya's engagement, there was one nagging thought in the back of her mind that she couldn't shake. Hunter. What she couldn't figure out was why she was so upset about him dating Amber. *Oh stop,* she told herself. *You don't have any claim on the man. You aren't even interested in him!* Yet, there he was, occupying her thoughts from time to time.

Her zombielike pace was interrupted when she accidentally bumped into someone. "Excuse me," she mumbled without looking up.

"No problem," she heard Hunter say.

She was immediately jerked out of her stupor when she heard his voice. Her face turned red with embarrassment. "Oh, Hunter, hi. I didn't see you there, sorry."

Hunter laughed. "It's all good. I'm surprised to see you up here," he said. "Are you all packed and ready for your trip?"

Jexi was almost frozen. "Um, we're getting there. We have raised the money we need. And as a matter of fact, can I talk to you for a minute?" She glanced around the room and saw Lindy watching. "Outside?" she added.

"Sure," Hunter agreed. "Is everything okay?"

"Yeah, just want to talk to you really quick, is all," Jexi said.

The two walked outside and stopped at the sidewalk on the side of the church.

"What's up?" Hunter asked. "You are acting a little strange."

Jexi looked at his face. His smile was as brilliant and his eyes as handsome as she remembered. Mentally she shook those thoughts away. She reminded herself that he was with Amber now and so she focused on what she wanted to say.

"Um, I wanted to thank you before we leave for Honduras next week. I know that you donated anonymously to our trip, and I know that it was a lot. I just wanted to say thank you. I really appreciate it. More than you know."

Hunter looked at the ground and rubbed the back of his head. "Well, yeah, that was supposed to stay anonymous," he said. "Did Lindy tell you?"

Jexi smiled up at him and batted her eyelashes. "I'll never tell. Let's just say, I am difficult to deny."

"That's no lie," Hunter replied, looking into her eyes.

Jexi quickly averted her gaze. "Please don't get anyone into trouble for telling me. It's really my fault. If I didn't thank you before we went, it would eat at me the whole trip."

Hunter chuckled. "Okay, it's alright. I forgive you for your nosiness and whoever told you. And you're welcome." He leaned over to hug her.

Jexi started to stiffen up because she wasn't sure she should be hugging the boyfriend of another girl. But after a second, she relaxed into the warm embrace. She wasn't sure how long they stood that way, and she really didn't care. This just felt so nice.

Suddenly, Hunter's cell phone rang and the two jumped apart as if lightning had struck them. Hunter fumbled for his phone and finally answered it. "Hi, Amber," he said.

Jexi heard Amber's shrill voice through the earpiece. "When are you coming over?" she asked.

Jexi stepped to the side and waved goodbye to Hunter as she walked back into the church.

Hunter responded to Amber as he watched Jexi walk away, inwardly wishing she wouldn't go. "We are no longer a couple, Amber. We broke up. I won't be coming over."

He heard Amber crying and sniffling. "I told you that I wanted to talk about things. You at least owe me that."

"No, Amber, I don't," Hunter replied. "I've already explained why I don't feel that we are compatible. I've prayed about this a lot, and I don't want to lead you on or allow you to think that we could be together. I'm sorry that you feel hurt, but we just won't work as a couple. I wish you the best." Hunter ended the call and walked slowly into the church.

CHAPTER TWO

Jessie navigated the heavy Kansas City traffic as they arrived in the late afternoon. "We probably should have timed this better to avoid rush hour," she commented.

Jexi shrugged, "Probably. But we really weren't thinking about the traffic when we were loading all of the supplies into the car. How are we going to get all of this to Honduras? We'll have to get to the airport super early to get all of this checked in."

"We will just have to pay a little extra for checked bags," Jessie answered. "I figured that into the costs, so we will be fine."

Jexi was relieved. *When am I going to get used to the idea that God is in even the smallest of details?* she mused with a smile.

They arrived safely at Jexi's parents' house and went inside. They sat down on the sofa and couch for a minute to catch their breath. "Are you going to the bookstore tonight?" Jessie asked.

"Yes, Shaun arranged a bit of a going-away party for us," Jexi explained. "I'd love for you to come too if you would."

"I'd be happy to," Jessie said. "What time do we need to be there?"

"It starts at seven." Jexi looked at her watch. "It's already six fifteen! I guess we should get moving."

Jessie groaned as she stood up from the couch. "This old body doesn't move as limberly as it used to," she joked. Jexi laughed with her as they walked out to the car.

The duo stopped at a fast-food restaurant to grab a bite to eat and then headed to the bookstore. It was difficult to locate a parking spot as the lot was almost full. When they walked inside, Jexi scanned the room to find Shaun. She smiled at the crowd. Having this many people in the building meant that Shaun was continuing to do well with holding live events and she was very happy for him.

She finally located Shaun in the backroom making final adjustments for the show. She rushed over to greet him. He hugged her and she introduced him to Aunt Jessie.

"Thank you for having us over tonight," Jessie said.

"It's nothing," Shaun answered. "I am thrilled to be able to help Jexi. I'm really proud of her."

Jexi's cheeks flushed a little. "Thanks, Shaun," she said.

Shaun looked at his watch. "Just about seven," he said. He looked at Jexi. "I have prepared for you to speak for a couple of minutes before the show starts. You'll be on in five."

Butterflies filled Jexi's stomach. She hadn't thought about speaking in front of so many people. But she was truly grateful, and she wanted them to know. She stood nervously by the stage with Jessie holding her hand.

After some time had passed, Shaun stepped up on the stage and attempted to get the crowd's attention. "Ladies and gentlemen, I know that many of you are here for our live show. That will begin in about five minutes. First, my former employee, Jexi Driscoll, is in the house tonight! She and her Aunt Jessie are leaving tomorrow for a mission trip in Honduras. We have had a collection jar at the front of the store for some time now and we would like to present Jexi and Jessie with two hundred dollars!"

The crowd clapped wildly as Jexi and Jessie stepped on stage. Jexi walked to Shaun, and he handed her an envelope. She turned to face the throng of people.

As she took the mic, her voice was soft and timid. "Thank you to everyone who has donated and prayed for us. We are so very thankful. You have been a great blessing from God and this money helps us minister to needy families in Honduras. Shaun didn't mention that HE personally donated several books for the students to use in their small school. He is far too humble to take any credit. Again, thank you."

The crowd erupted in cheers and applause and Jessie and Jexi walked off the stage. Shaun introduced the band and the show began.

As Jexi was walking toward the front of the store, she felt a tap on her shoulder. She turned around to see a gentleman and his wife standing there. The gentleman had a check in his extended hand. "My wife and I want to help you with funding for your next trip to Honduras," he said.

Jexi shot a puzzled look at Jessie. "But I don't have another trip planned," she protested. "Thank you so much for your generosity, but God has already met our needs for this one."

The gentleman looked at his wife who took the check from him. She moved closer to Jexi. "God has told us that you will be going back and that you will need the money. He told us that you will be doing great work there. We want to be obedient and help support His kingdom."

Jexi was shocked. She couldn't think of how in the world this couple seemed to think that she would return to Honduras. She had no plans to go again after this trip. She stood speechless.

Jessie reached out and took the check. She then hugged the woman with tears in her eyes. "Thank you for your kindness and obedience," Jessie told her. "We wouldn't dare steal your blessing."

The couple clasped hands with Jessie and then they walked away. Jexi was baffled. "What does that mean, Aunt Jessie? I don't really understand what just happened."

Jessie smiled and giggled a bit. "Oh, child, you have so much to learn. That couple was in tune with the Holy Spirit. He gave them instructions and they obeyed. By allowing them to give us the money, they will be blessed by God for following His prompting."

"But they don't know us. They didn't know we would be here, and we haven't even discussed another trip," Jexi stated.

"None of that matters a bit," Jessie responded. "For them, it was doing as the Holy Spirit asked them to. It doesn't matter if we know them or if we have another trip planned. God knows more than we do, that's for sure!"

Jexi reached for the check and looked at the amount. "Holy buckets! It's a thousand dollars!" she yelled.

"Praise Jesus!" Jessie exclaimed.

Jexi understood a little bit of what Jessie was explaining but was still so befuddled by what had just happened. Jessie was right. She really did have a lot to learn. God was enormous. God was mysterious. God was magnificent. And He did this for insignificant HER. She stared at the check for a good while as tears rolled down her cheeks.

The rest of the evening was a blur for Jexi. She and Jessie mingled a little bit and received a couple more donations. It was getting late and they had an early morning ahead. They said goodbye and made final plans with Shaun. The drive home was quiet and uneventful.

By the time they arrived at Jexi's parents' house, they were both ready for bed. Jexi was exhausted but in a good way. She swelled with joy knowing that God loved her in a way she had never known. She drifted off to sleep filled with a warmth that she never wanted to lose.

CHAPTER THREE

Shaun rang the doorbell early the next morning. The three gathered up all their belongings and loaded the car. At the airport, checking in the extra boxes was not a problem, just as Aunt Jessie had predicted. Once they reached the waiting area for their flight, Jexi quickly called Shaya before the plane took off.

"Hi, world traveler!" Shaya said when she picked up the phone. "Is everything going okay?"

"Yes!" Jexi replied excitedly. "It's all going so smoothly! I can totally see God's hand at work in all of this!"

Shaya smiled. It was so exciting watching a new believer learn about God and grow closer to Him. "That's great!" she replied. "I'm so happy for you!"

"I'm sorry I haven't been able to help a lot with your wedding planning," Jexi said.

"It's okay!" Shaya responded. "I've already told you that! I know this trip is a huge deal and you had a lot to get ready for. Stop apologizing."

Jexi giggled. "Okay, thanks. But I have about fifteen minutes before we start boarding, so you can fill me in on what you've done lately since we haven't had a lot of time to talk."

"Well, you already know my colors are blue and blush. Mom and I were able to find tablecloths a few days ago! They are the perfect colors. Ben has his suit rented and found the perfect suits for the groomsmen. OH! I almost forgot the biggest news. My dad is actually coming and is going to give me away."

"WHAT?!" Jexi exclaimed.

"I know, right?!" responded Shaya. "I've talked with him several times since he called at Christmas, and he wants to do this! I am so pumped!"

"Shaya, why didn't you tell me you have been talking to your dad?" Jexi asked in confusion.

"You've been so busy prepping for Honduras," Shaya answered. "I didn't want to bother you."

"I know," Jexi said, "but you are still my best friend, and you can talk to me anytime, no matter what I'm doing! This is HUGE news."

Aunt Jessie pulled out her earbuds, leaned over, and whispered, "What's going on? What is she talking about that has you all rattled?"

Jexi pulled the phone away from her ear. "She's been talking to her dad!" she told Jessie. "And she hadn't told me!"

Jessie looked surprised. "Well, we have been busy. She probably didn't want to bother you."

Jexi looked shocked. "Don't take her side!" she said. "And daddy dearest is giving her away at the wedding."

Jessie held her hands like she was surrendering, "Okay, okay, I'll stay out of it. But tell her I said congratulations."

Jexi heard Shaya in her ear, "Hey, you will have three weeks to talk to Jessie. You only have fifteen minutes with me."

Jexi put the phone back to her ear. "I know, sorry," she said. "Tell me more!"

Shaya continued. "So, we have the suit picked out for Dad too. Mom has three dresses she is considering; she can't make up her mind. I honestly don't know why she's making such a fuss. It's just a simple little wedding. I keep telling her she will be beautiful in any of the three."

Jexi laughed. "If I know your mom, she wants to be perfect for your big day. And I can't blame her. It's sweet."

Shaya sighed, "Yeah, sweet, but also a little annoying. But I guess she has time to decide. We have an appointment with the seamstress a few days after you return to check on the dress alterations. Whatever you do, don't lose or gain any weight while you are gone!"

"I'll do my best," Jexi said. "But I make no promises. From what Jessie has told me Anita is an excellent cook and will be offended if I don't eat what she prepares."

Shaya laughed. "Jex, I'm proud of you, and I am jealous that you are going to have this wonderful adventure without me. Maybe someday Ben and I can take a mission trip."

"Don't make it weird," Jexi replied, laughing.

Shaya laughed. "I'm just saying that I'd love to go on a mission trip. And perhaps I am going to miss you."

"Okay, it's weird now," Jexi said. She giggled. "Truth be told, I'll miss you too." She heard the announcement that boarding would begin in a moment. "Shaya, it's almost time to get on the plane. I need to go. At the risk of making it weirder, I love you and am glad you're my bestie. You know, just in case something happens to me."

Shaya sniffled. "Love you too," she said.

"Are you crying?" Jexi asked."

"Allergies!" Shaya quipped.

"Right," Jexi said sarcastically. "My allergies are bothering me too. See you in three weeks!"

"Bye," said Shaya. "Have a good flight!"

Jexi and Jessie got in line to board the plane. Jexi was filled with excitement and anxiety. She never imagined that she would be leaving the country, much less going on a mission trip.

When they were in their seats, and the plane was taxiing to the runway, Jexi thought about how she had ended up on a flight to Honduras. In the past eight months, her life had changed so much. Eight months ago, she was about to be Mrs. Ludovico, but Brennan had stood her up on their wedding day. Without her best friend, she would have been homeless and unemployed. Shaya had accompanied her on the cruise that would have been her honeymoon. That was the cruise that reunited Shaya with Ben, the love of her life. It was also the cruise where Jexi met Hunter.

Hunter had provided her with a much-needed distraction from her recent debacle of a life, but that's all it was. She couldn't figure out why he was on her mind so much. But before she could figure out any serious feelings that she might have, he had moved on with Amber.

Then came the job at the bookstore that led to her wonderful friend, Shaun, and then the big move to Baxter Springs where she had decided to get a fresh start. It was fun rooming with Shaya and working at Aunt Katie's diner. It was there, at a church in Baxter Springs, that she had encountered God and accepted Him as her Lord and Savior. This ultimately led to her heeding the call to head to Honduras.

This was not where she thought she would be in life, but this was also where she wanted to be right now. She felt, for the first time in her life, that she was following God's will, rather than her own.

Jexi closed her eyes and let the hum of the plane lull her to sleep. She was mentally and physically drained and knew she needed to rest up for what she was about to do.

The bump and squeal of the landing gear on the runway jerked her out of her slumber. She looked over and noticed Jessie was still asleep. She nudged her and wondered how she slept through that noise. Jessie slowly opened her eyes and questioned, "Why are you bothering me in the middle of a great dream? I was riding horses on the beach with the mustache version of Sam Elliot."

"We landed," Jexi told her as she giggled and rolled her eyes. "We need to get to the gate for our next flight. And the Miami Airport is bound to be crowded."

Jessie sat straight up. "Oh, yes. Time to get to business. We don't have a lot of time between flights. I'll finish my jaunt with Sam later."

Jexi laughed and pulled her carry-on out from under her seat. "Aunt Jessie, you're a riot. Always keeping me on my toes."

Jessie also laughed and collected her carry-on. "You've got Hunter to dream of, I have my Sam."

"Aunt Jessie!" Jexi exclaimed. "I don't dream of Hunter! Besides, he's dating Amber. Oh look, the line is moving. Let's go." She was thankful for the distraction.

They disembarked and swiftly headed toward the gate of their next flight. By the time they were seated, they were both out of breath.

"Whew," Jessie gasped. "We made it. Looks like they'll be loading in about fifteen minutes."

Jexi nodded. "I'm sure glad we didn't miss the flight. That would be a nightmare."

Jessie got a knowing look on her face and began, "Speaking of nightmares, you mentioned that Amber girl earlier. That is the true nightmare right there. Although I shouldn't be a-gossipin'."

"What do you mean by *nightmare*?" Jexi asked. "You can't just say something like that and then stop! Explain!"

Jessie looked skyward. "Forgive me for gossipin', Lord." She then looked back at Jexi. "Well, that little lady is a phony through and through. Hunter won't be staying with her very long at all."

Jexi's eyes widened. "Phony?" she inquired. "Like how?"

"Well, looks can be deceiving, you know," Jessie replied. "By all appearances, she's a good Christian girl. But I've known her for a long time and I have seen some things that make me wonder. For example, she volunteers in the children's ministry. But I've heard her on several occasions saying how she can't stand the little *snot-nosed brats.* Her words, not mine." Jessie paused to dig through her purse for some hand sanitizer. "I feel gross. Want some?" She held out the sanitizer for Jexi.

"NO! I don't want sanitizer. I want to know more about Amber," Jexi insisted.

"Oh alright. I don't think she can be trusted. While she'll be sweet as pie to your face, she'll just as soon talk about you behind your back," Jessie explained. "Plus, she's tried to snag every single man in town, including Ben. But since Ben didn't give her the time of day, she set her sights on Hunter. Looks like she caught him. For now, anyway."

Jexi looked at Jessie, "You don't think they will last, is that what you mean?"

Jessie laughed, "Child, I'm on the verge of being an old woman and have seen many young relationships get together and get torn apart. I can see when a couple has what it takes to make it. Like Shaya and Ben. They've got that special something. Hunter's no dummy. He will see right through Amber. It's just a matter of time before her true self will show. And Hunter won't like what he will see."

Jexi leaned back in her chair. "Hmm, that's interesting."

"What I'm saying is that you still have a shot with him," Jessie added.

"Who says I want a shot with him?" Jexi asked. "It's not like that with us. We are just friends."

Jessie pursed her lips. "Mm-hmm," she said in a disbelieving way. "Sure you are. I've seen the way he looks at you."

"Jessie, really, there's nothing there," Jexi protested. But already her cheeks were beginning to warm with blush. She turned away.

Jessie reached over and patted her arm. "Sugar, you don't need to protest. I see it in your eyes, and I sense it in your heart."

Jexi didn't respond. She wasn't sure what she would say anyhow. She simply squeezed Jessie's hand and smiled. Aunt Jessie wasn't really her aunt, but she sure felt like family.

CHAPTER FOUR

The flight from Miami to Tegucigalpa seemed to go quicker than Jexi thought it would. As they exited the plane, they saw a couple holding signs with their names. "Oh, those two," Jessie mentioned. "They are so funny. Like I needed a sign!"

Jessie waved and then ran right to them with Jexi in tow. She hugged them both at once and then pulled away. She waved her hand toward Jexi and introduced her. "Ken, Sharon, please meet Jexi Driscoll. Jexi, this is Ken and Sharon VanLiew, the mission directors and liaisons."

Jexi extended her arm to shake hands with Sharon first. Sharon laughed and embraced her. "We are friends already! We hug around here!"

Jexi stepped back and looked toward Ken. He moved to her and hugged her. "Me too," Ken said.

Jessie spoke up, "We need to get our luggage and boxes. Oh, Sharon, you are going to love the things we were able to collect!"

"It doesn't matter if I love it, will the kids love it?" Sharon asked.

"Yes, they will!" Jessie answered. "Jexi was able to score a couple of boxes of books for the children in the village."

The group located the baggage claim area and retrieved the suitcases and boxes of donations. They worked together to get it to Ken and Sharon's van and get it loaded. Then they all climbed into the van for the four-hour ride to the tiny town of Aldea Gracia.

Sharon talked with Jessie for much of the ride and Jexi listened to absorb as much information as she could. She was already aware of one of the families in Aldea Gracia, and she couldn't wait to meet them. Sharon was telling Jessie of recent events going on in the village.

Juan Carlos, the unspoken leader of the families, was having a hard time tilling the land and planting crops successfully. His wife, Angelica, hadn't been feeling well and it was difficult to tend to her and the farming responsibilities. Fortunately, Carlos and Anita, Juan Carlos's parents, could help tend to Angelica. But there were also the four younger children to consider. The two older children were tremendously helpful. JC, Juan Carlos's eldest son, and Carlita, his eldest daughter, were old enough to take on a lot of the village responsibilities. With little income and such poverty-stricken conditions, the families needed help.

"That's why we are here," said Jessie. "We are ready to work for the next three weeks. We should be able to help get the seeds in the ground to start the growing season."

"Their little church that they also use as the schoolhouse is in desperate need of painting," Ken mentioned. "We have the paint and the brushes. How are your painting skills?"

"Spectacular!" Jessie said. "If I had more time, I would paint a mural on the interior wall," she added with confidence.

Jexi couldn't imagine what it would be like to see a small village. She looked out the window as the van drove and saw the big city atmosphere turn into nothing but countryside. After a while, she began to see some resemblance to civilization. But this was nothing like the civilization she knew. What she saw broke her heart into a million pieces. The buildings were mere shacks, rickety, and lacking amenities. There were cutouts for windows but no glass to separate the outside and inside. A few of them had blankets covering the openings. Jexi wondered how the homes were protected from the elements.

All of a sudden, she heard Ken say, "We're home!"

Jexi piled out of the van and looked around. She wasn't sure that she could believe her eyes. They were standing in some sort of outdoor commons area. She could see the small building that the village used as the church and schoolhouse and noticed that it too was in a bad state of disrepair. The next thing she saw was people running toward them and greeting Ken, Sharon, and Jessie. They were smiling and happy to see their old friends. Jexi looked at the villagers and noticed that most were barefoot. The clothes they wore were ones that had been donated, and they were beginning to wear out. Many of the children were dirty and their hair was uncombed. Despite the circumstances, all she could see were the friends greeting each other and laughing. She did not see even a hint of despair on any of their faces.

Jexi waited, standing in the mix, for an introduction. She didn't know what else to do. She hadn't realized that the group had moved into her space and began to hug her as well.

She snapped out of her fog as Jessie was trying to introduce her to everyone. She was hugging strangers, but it didn't feel weird at all. They were thrilled to have her visit their tiny community and several were offering to take her on a tour.

"Juan Carlos, will you help unload the supplies and luggage from the van?" Ken asked.

"*Si,* senor," Juan Carlos answered. He added in broken English, "We will help." He motioned to a few of the other men.

The two men along with JC and some other men from the village went to the van to unload the cargo. The children began to gather around the boxes, eager to see what was inside. Jessie walked to one of the boxes and asked for a crowbar. JC brought her one and she cracked the box open.

"You have books for school now!" she announced to the children. The children erupted in cheers and applause and ran around the box laughing. Jexi had never seen anyone express such joy over receiving books. "We also brought pencils and paper and other school supplies!" Jessie continued.

While Jexi watched them open each box and reveal the treasures hidden inside, her eyes began to water. These people were so excited because they had been given shoes. They acted as if someone had just handed them a million dollars instead of mere shoes. Jexi couldn't hold back the tears that began to trickle down her face. At that moment she was struck by how privileged and selfish she had been and how many blessings God had really given to her. She realized that she had not been thankful for very much, just taking simple pleasures for granted. She vowed right there to always show gratitude, for every tiny little thing in her life.

Jessie walked over to Jexi and put her arm around her. "It really hits you the first time, doesn't it?" she asked.

Jexi nodded and began to cry a bit more. "I just wasn't . . . I didn't know . . . ."

"It's okay, hon," Jessie said. "It happens to everyone when they first see the reality of life here. Give it a moment to sink in."

Jexi looked down to see a tiny, tanned face looking up at her. The little girl smiled and gestured to Jexi to bend down to her level. Jexi did as the little girl requested. The girl reached her small hand to Jexi's face and wiped away her tears. "No sad," she said.

Jexi reached for the little girl's hand and rested it against her face. A slow smile crept in, and Jexi could feel her sadness dissipate. "No sad," Jexi replied.

"This is Natalia," Jessie explained. "She is Juan Carlos and Angelica's youngest."

Jexi picked the little girl up in her arms and hugged her tightly. "Gracias," she whispered to Natalia and the small one beamed with joy. She turned to Jessie. "This is incredible," she said.

Jessie smiled. "I'll leave you two for now. I need to go help get supplies put away."

"Do you need me to come help?" Jexi asked.

"No, no," Jessie answered. "Stay here with the children. They love having visitors." Jessie walked away.

Jexi sat down on the ground and several small kids came to see her. Juan Carlos' daughter, Sophia, reached into Jexi's long black hair and began twisting it into a braid. Another sang her a song and tried to get Jexi to sing along. Jexi did her best to catch onto the words, and she hummed when she did not know what to sing. Natalia sat contently in Jexi's lap and refused to move. Jexi wept tears of joy.

Natalia touched her face again and said, "No sad."

Jexi smiled down at her and said, "Happy tears."

Natalia looked confused. "Happy sad?" she asked.

Jexi giggled and nodded. "Happy sad," she answered. That seemed to satisfy Natalia as she continued to wipe tears from Jexi's face. Jexi had never experienced instant love before, but she knew that's what was happening here. Her heart had never been so full.

Eventually, the adults returned and led Jessie and Jexi to their sleeping quarters so they could get settled. Juan Carlos said something to Jessie in Spanish that Jexi did not understand, and Jessie replied in Spanish. Juan Carlos turned and left them alone.

"What did he say?" asked Jexi.

"He said dinner would be served in an hour if we want to rest for a while," Jessie replied. "We'll all eat together around the wood fire grill in the commons area.

"Oh, thank goodness! A nap and a meal are my favorite combo!" Jexi stated.

The two women settled in and crawled into the twin-sized beds for a quick nap. It wasn't difficult to fall asleep because they were both worn out to the core.

They woke after a while to hear the noise of the villagers outside their quarters. They sleepily joined the excitement looming around them.

Anita, Angelica, and a few other village women were preparing the food and placing the plates and utensils on a table near the grill. When they were finished, Anita announced dinner was ready, and Juan Carlos blessed the food with mixed Spanish and English.

Jexi looked around and saw a few chairs, benches, and blankets that had been brought out for the meal. She was in awe of the way these villagers all worked seamlessly together, like one big family.

"You were right. That was one stellar meal. Anita is a great cook," Jexi said to Jessie.

Jessie turned to Anita and said something to her in Spanish. Anita smiled and rushed over to hug Jexi.

Jexi looked at Jessie with confusion. "What is this about?" she asked with Anita's arms wrapped around her.

"I told her what you said about her cooking," Jessie said. "She is thrilled that you enjoyed the meal."

Jexi smiled at Anita. "Gracias," she said as she rubbed her stomach. "Very yummy!"

Anita squeezed her and then went to talk to Juan Carlos. Jexi watched the villagers interact, laugh, and talk. She wasn't scared or nervous anymore. As a matter of fact, she knew that she was smack dab in the middle of God's will for her life and she couldn't have been happier.

CHAPTER FIVE

The time in Honduras seemed to fly by as Jexi kept herself busy. She helped with painting the school and other various chores. She felt more and more at home as she got to know Juan Carlos, Angelica, and the rest of the villagers better. Yet one thing still baffled her; how these people could be so joyful amid their impoverished surroundings.

She had talked with Aunt Jessie about this once, to gain understanding. Jessie tried to explain to her that, in their opinion, these individuals were lacking in so much. But in the opinion of the residents, they were abundantly blessed.

Jexi asked, "How is it that they feel blessed? They don't have electricity but maybe a couple of hours a day. They don't have enough clothing or enough food. They walk to the river and haul water back every day, which isn't even safe to drink. I guess I don't understand."

Jessie answered, "They don't look at it that way. What they see is a freshwater source for them to get water daily. They see that God has blessed them with land that will grow crops. They don't have to worry about a lot of clothing because they don't go to very many places. When you look at something with a 'glass half full' mentality, you start to see your circumstances completely differently. They have everything they need."

Jexi pondered what she heard. She did her best to see the situation from a positive point of view. As she did, she slowly began to comprehend why there was so much joy here.

Aunt Jessie continued talking. "We were sent here to share with them the teachings of Christ. We have given them Bibles to read and told them about the love of God. They get their joy from knowing that

God will take care of their every need. They don't get angry at Him because He did not provide something frivolous they wanted."

Jexi felt a pang of guilt. She had been quite angry at God for not giving her Brennan. She had been wrong in expecting God to be at her beck and call, giving her everything she desired. "I see," she said to Jessie. "I think I'm getting it. This is truly remarkable."

"God's ways are nothing less than remarkable, honey," Jessie replied. "Juan Carlos and the others in the village have learned about God and what He wants for their lives. They seek to spend every moment walking in His will for them and because of this, God showers them with blessings, and they are extremely thankful. One of their favorite verses here is First Thessalonians five, eighteen. It says, 'Give thanks in all circumstances; for this is the will of God in Christ Jesus for you.' They strive to live by this verse."

After that conversation, Jexi decided that she would do her best to live her life in the same manner. God had already shown her so much grace. She now knew that being within His will for her was the best place to be. Isn't that why she was here, in Honduras?

She had become particularly close with the children, especially Natalia. That little girl had clung close to Jexi and followed her almost everywhere. Natalia was so excited when she tried to teach Jexi some Honduran songs and games. Diego, the fourteen-year-old son of Juan Carlos and Angelica, had expressed his undying love for Jexi and had asked her to be his wife. She felt bad for denying his request because she could see he really thought he was in love with her. The memory made her smile. Carlita and Jexi had shared some heartfelt conversations and had bonded deeply. Dante and Sophia enjoyed listening to her stories about the United States. She was truly going to miss them and everything about this place.

Before she knew it, their last night in Honduras was upon them. The village all came together again for a large party and feast. This time, Jexi marveled at how generous they were. She knew that there was not a lot of food to share and putting out this much meant that most of them would have to go without for a meal.

The group laughed, sang, and danced after dinner. Jexi joined in wholeheartedly and had one of the best evenings of her life. That night as they prepared for bed, she told Jessie that she wanted to come back as soon as possible.

Jessie laughed. "I thought you didn't have another trip planned. Don't you remember?"

Jexi giggled also. "I didn't! But evidently, God did. I guess I may have spoken too soon. I had no idea I would fall in love with this place. God knew how I would feel even before I did. He is so amazing! The weird part is that I haven't really missed my life in the States. The people, yes, but not my stuff."

Jessie wrapped her arm around Jexi's shoulder. "And this is just the beginning, child," she said as she winked at her. "Now, we have an early flight to catch in the morning. We best get some shut-eye."

Jexi whined. "I don't want this night to be over," she complained. "But at least now I know I will return!"

When the alarm clock rang at four AM the next morning, Jexi groaned. She rolled over and smacked the clock to shut off the noise. "It's so early," she whined softly. She got out of bed and looked over at Jessie who was beginning to stir in her bed. They both dressed for the day and packed the last of their belongings.

Ken and Sharon were expected to arrive at approximately five AM to take them to the airport. Jexi and Jessie were eating some breakfast that Anita had prepared for them when Jessie noticed a truck driving slowly around the perimeter of the village. She tapped Jexi and said, "Ken and Sharon are here. Let's get moving."

Jexi said thank you to Anita who enveloped her in a bear hug. She looked up to see the truck suspiciously moving at a crawl. "I wonder what they're doing," she pondered aloud. "They don't seem to be in a hurry at all."

Jessie looked a little longer in the direction of the truck and then shrugged. "Guess that isn't them. Must be a utility truck," she ventured as she turned to set her luggage down.

"Um, Aunt Jessie, I don't think most utility men drive around in the back of trucks carrying guns, do you?" Jexi asked nervously.

Jessie whipped back around. "Guns?!" she asked.

"Yeah," Jexi whispered. "There are like three or four men standing in the back holding guns."

Anita did not seem the least bit fazed. She busied herself, cleaning up the breakfast dishes.

Jessie walked toward Juan Carlos's cabin. "Juan Carlos?" she called.

Juan Carlos appeared in the doorway. *"Si,* senora, good morning."

"Jexi and I just saw a truck on the edge of the village and there were men in the truck with guns. What's going on?"

Juan Carlos waved his hand and answered, "We see them all the time. They come here and drive around and then go."

"They haven't bothered you?" asked Jessie. "Who are they?"

Juan Carlos shook his head. "No, they do not bother. We do not know them, but someone buy land around." He gestured with his hand to indicate the land all around the village. "We get letter from a new owner. They want us to leave," he added in his broken English.

Jessie gasped. "Juan Carlos! Why didn't you say something?!" she shrieked. "Maybe we can help!"

Juan Carlos shrugged. "This my land. They no bother us. So, all is okay," he answered.

Jessie calmed some. "Can I see the letter?" she asked.

Juan Carlos went into his home and came back carrying the letter. Because it was in Spanish, he had to translate most of it for Jessie.

"Oh, that's scary!" Jessie exclaimed. "They really want this land, don't they? But we know that this threat cannot be backed with anything because of the contract you all signed with the previous landowner. Mr. Henderson made sure to deed this land to you and keep it in the contract so that you could stay here on your little plot. Along with several other villages."

Juan Carlos looked puzzled. *"Que?"* he asked.

Jessie explained. "When Mr. Henderson bought the land, he allowed you to stay, do you remember?"

Juan Carlos nodded, *"Si."*

"That means, legally, he put in the documents that your village, Aldea Gracia, holds ownership of this part of the land, and any new owner has to let you stay," Jessie continued.

Juan Carlos smiled. "So, we stay?" he asked.

"Yep," answered Jessie.

Ken and Sharon's van pulled into the village. Juan Carlos hugged Jessie before she turned to go. "Gracias, *mi amiga,*" he said.

"De nada," responded Jessie as she returned the hug. "Until next time, my friend. I will see you soon."

Jessie and Jexi said their goodbyes and gave lots of final hugs. They loaded their items into the van and climbed in. The whole village had come to see them leave and everyone was waving. Jexi even found herself crying as she waved goodbye.

Ken smiled at Jexi. "They get into your heart, don't they?" She nodded as she wiped her eyes.

On the four-hour trip to the airport, Jessie inquired about the owner of the land that surrounded the village.

"His name is Stan McGreggor," said Sharon. "We haven't had a lot of interaction with him, and I'd prefer to keep it that way. He is a gruff, gruff man."

"He is extremely wealthy and loves to use his financial means to influence others," Ken added. "Two of the villages have accepted his offer to move off the land. For a price, of course."

"He sounds like a scary guy. He can't make them leave, can he?" asked Jexi.

"No," Ken answered. "Mike Henderson made it a stipulation of buying that land that the villages get to stay right where they are. Each village takes up no more than nine or ten acres each and the land, as a whole, totals a thousand acres. There is plenty of land for the owner to cultivate."

"Why did Mr. Henderson sell the land to such an unscrupulous man?" Jexi asked.

Sharon looked at Jexi. "Mike didn't sell the land. He passed away and didn't have any dependents or a will. The land was auctioned off to a new owner."

"Oh, how sad," Jexi replied.

"We have heard rumors that the new owner has powerful connections with organized crime if you know what I mean," said Sharon. "But legally, Juan Carlos and the village are safe, even though Stan McGreggor has tried to use illegal means to extricate the villages. That's why a couple of villages have already left. We just need to pray about the whole thing. God is in control, and He will protect them."

CHAPTER SIX

Jexi couldn't believe her eyes as she and Jessie walked off the plane in Kansas City. Ben and Shaya stood at the gate waving excitedly. She ran to Shaya and wrapped her in a hug.

"What are you doing here?" she asked Shaya.

"We wanted to surprise you!" Shaya answered. "We wanted to come and see some friends who had heard about our engagement, so we thought that we would just pick you two up from the airport! You know, kill-two-birds-with-one-stone type of thing," she turned slightly and opened her arms for another hug. "Hey, Aunt Jessie."

"You, sweet girl," Jessie said as she embraced Shaya. "That was thoughtful of you!"

Jexi agreed. "Yeah, it is!"

"We also thought it might save you the cost of an Uber," Ben added. He pointed to Shaya. "But to be honest, your girl here was jumping out of her skin to see you."

"I might have missed you a little," Shaya admitted. "But don't make it weird."

Jexi turned toward the baggage claim area. "We have a few bags to pick up," she said.

The group walked and chatted as they headed to pick up their suitcases.

Shaya said eagerly to Jexi, "I want you to tell me everything! I can't wait to hear how your first mission trip went!"

Jexi snickered at her excitement. "I promise to give you every detail. But not right now. It's too noisy and chaotic to talk. Let's get home first, okay?"

Shaya lifted her shoulders. "Okay," she agreed. "But can you, at least, tell me if you had a good time?"

"I had an amazing time," Jexi gushed, smiling. "It was way beyond my greatest expectations!"

The group gathered the luggage and got it loaded into the car. Shaya and Aunt Jessie chatted on the way to Jexi's parents' house. Jexi laid her head back on the headrest and closed her eyes. She was so tired but felt like she was on top of the world. She started to doze just a bit as the car moved through Kansas City. She wanted to tell Shaya all about her adventure, but it would have to wait. Sleep had become a top priority.

Back in Baxter Springs, life quickly returned to normalcy. Jexi went back to working at the diner and attending church regularly. She thought often of Honduras and the little village of people who had stolen her heart. Occasionally she would get a text from Carlita filling her in on happenings in Aldea Gracia and Natalia's milestones.

In one of their conversations, Carlita delivered some very exciting news.

"Guess what?" she texted. *"Mom is pregnant!"*

Jexi squealed and typed into her phone, *"That is so exciting! Tell your parents that I say congratulations!"* Jexi was excited to hear about the baby but was also concerned that Juan Carlos and Angelica would now have seven children to care for. She thought to herself, *how are they going to feed another one when they barely survive as it is?* She stopped herself. *God will provide.*

One Sunday afternoon, after being home for three weeks, a concerned Aunt Jessie burst through Attie's door, where Attie and the girls were finishing up lunch. "Pray for Aldea Gracia!" she exclaimed.

"What's wrong?" asked Jexi.

"Their water supply has been blocked," Jessie explained. "They don't know who did it, but someone has put up a thick fence blocking their path to the water. Juan Carlos tore it down twice, but by the next day, it was up again. They are having to go out of their way three miles extra to get fresh water."

Jexi's anger burned. "I'll bet it's that McGreggor," she murmured.

"Can they dig a well?" Attie asked.

"Yes," Jessie answered, "but it's a lot of work. They have been trying to put a well in the center of the village, but they have faced several setbacks. The water is very deep underground, and it takes a long time to reach it. They must create a proper wall to keep the walls of the well from collapsing in on itself, which has happened a few times. Another problem they are experiencing is that they can't afford enough cement for the walls."

Jexi thought for a moment and quietly stated, "We need to go back and help. How soon can we leave? Can we take cement with us?"

Jessie let out a whoop. "My thoughts exactly, child!" she yelled.

Shaya, who had been listening without input until now, slowly added, "But I'm getting married in a week. What about the wedding? You aren't planning to take off before my wedding, are you?"

Jexi stopped. "No, of course not. I'd never miss being my best friend's maid of honor. We'll just go after the wedding." She paused and turned to Jessie in amazement. "The guy in Kansas City donated money for a second trip! WOW! I had no idea!"

Jessie laughed, "No, but God did!" she answered.

"What man are you ladies talking about?" asked Attie.

"This is one of the most incredible things!" Jexi said with wonder. "The night before we left, a man wanted to donate money and said that we would need it for our second trip. I tried to tell him that we didn't have a second trip planned, but he insisted that I take the money! I can't believe that God told him to donate so many weeks before we even knew that we would be going back!"

Jessie grabbed her wallet and pulled out a check. "It's right here. I forgot all about it. Look, one thousand dollars. I need to get this to the bank!"

Attie cheered. "I love watching our God in action!" she yelled.

Jessie hugged her. "Me too, sis! Me too!"

Jexi immediately looked at Jessie and said, "That is only half the money we need. I guess we'd better get to fundraising!"

"That will be enough for our plane tickets. We also have a little left over from the last trip. God will work out the rest. He always does," Jessie replied. "I have an idea. Let me send an email to the church congregation and see if we can get help."

Shaya looked between Jessie and Jexi. "I really wish I could go with you, guys, but Ben and I will be on our honeymoon."

"Enjoy your honeymoon," Jexi said and then she laughed. "Who knows, maybe we'll go down for a third time someday!"

That night, Jexi prayed hard for the villagers in Aldea Gracia. She lifted each of the members of Juan Carlos's family up to God and asked Him to protect them and care for them. She had grown to care very deeply for these people, and it ripped her apart that she couldn't be with them at this very moment.

The following day, Jexi went to Jessie's house to finalize the travel details. Jexi loved Jessie's house. It was the most eccentric home she'd ever seen and safe to say that it was the most creative structure in the whole town. It was made of stone and decorated with butterflies and fairies on the bottom half. The top half of the house was made of light blue cedar shake siding. The front door and the windowsills were painted a sunny yellow. The yard was filled with Jessie's creations, including many sizes and shapes of painted rocks. There was also a hummingbird-and-butterfly garden adorned with benches and feeders.

Jexi parked her car and walked up the cobblestone path to Jessie's front door. She lifted the large, white seashell doorknocker and tapped it three times. Jessie swung the door open before Jexi had gotten her hand off the knocker.

"Wow, you must have been waiting by the door!" Jexi exclaimed.

Jessie laughed. "What can I say, I'm excited. I already have my computer loaded with flight choices. We can leave two days after Shaya and Ben's wedding."

They were able to get plane tickets booked and Jessie was about to contact Ken and Sharon to arrange transportation from the airport when her phone chirped. Jessie looked at her phone and commented, "It's from Lindy at the church." As she opened her texting application, she added, "I wonder what she wants."

Silence filled the room for a moment as Jessie read the text from Lindy. Then she jumped up off the couch and hollered, "We already have donations waiting for us at the church!"

Jexi's jaw dropped. "Really?!" she asked in disbelief. "After not even a full day?"

Jessie smiled and winked at Jexi. "When God has plans for us, He also provides a way to make those plans happen. Have you forgotten that already?"

Jexi smiled. "I'm still adjusting, I guess," she said.

"Come on," Jessie said. "Let's go up to the church to gather those donations."

Jexi checked her watch. "I have a shift at the diner later this afternoon, but I have some time."

Jessie drove them to the church, and they walked into the office to visit Lindy. She handed them several envelopes and mentioned that there had been a huge response to Jessie's email the previous day.

"Thank you so much, Lindy!" Jexi said. "We knew God would provide."

Jessie rolled her eyes. "One of us did, anyway."

A male voice sounded from behind them, "I'm so glad I ran into you two."

They turned around and saw Hunter standing in the office doorway. Jessie gave him a puzzled look. "You were looking for us?" she asked.

Hunter grinned. "Yes. I wanted to ask you if there was any more space available on that trip you're taking. I'd like to join you."

"We'd love to have you come with us!" Jessie replied. "But we've already booked our tickets, so I can't promise that you'll sit next to us or even be on the same flight. Don't let that stop you though. The more strong young men we have available to help with that well, the better! Our flight leaves two days after Shaya's wedding on the twenty-seventh. Stop by the house and I'll print our flight information for you.

Jexi stood in shocked silence. This was a mixed blessing. She knew that it would be so helpful to have him help with the well. But personally, she was not sure that she could work so closely with Hunter. *What should I do?* she wondered. *Should I convince him not to come? I mean, I can't breathe right when he is near, and he is still in a relationship with Amber. Lord, what do I do?*

"What do you think, Jexi?" Jessie asked.

"Huh? I'm sorry. What were you asking?" Jexi said.

Hunter smiled at Jexi. "Are you okay? You look pale."

"Umm, yeah, sure," Jexi stammered. "I'm just overwhelmed by the, uh, generosity of people and stuff." She thought to herself, *I hope that sounded convincing.* Then she asked, "Don't you have work or something? Won't it be hard to get time off?"

"I have tons of vacation time accrued," Hunter answered. "They won't even miss me."

"Will Amber be coming, too?" Jexi asked.

Hunter looked at her with surprise on his face. "Amber? Why would she be coming with us?"

Jexi faltered just a little. "Isn't she your girlfriend?"

"We broke up a couple of months ago," Hunter replied. "She wasn't the one for me."

"Oh," Jexi said. "I'm sorry to hear that."

"Don't be sorry," said Hunter. "I'm glad I found out that we aren't compatible sooner rather than later . . . if you know what I mean."

CHAPTER SEVEN

Shaya's wedding day was upon them. Shaya's tastes had always been unique, and her wedding definitely reflected this. The morning wedding was scheduled to be held at Ben's Uncle and Aunt's farm. They had gone out the day before to decorate the area near the fishing pond where the ceremony would take place. Ben had built a small, adorable gazebo that stood near the water. The girls had added a feminine touch by wrapping the wood beams in blue tulle and garlands of blush-colored flowers. Rented white folding chairs had been placed in rows on either side of a blue runner, what would be the aisle.

On the north side of the pond, there was a very large tent that stood above several tables. The tables were covered with tablecloths and decorated with simple flower arrangements. Attie had requested fancy, ornate centerpieces but Shaya wanted the focus to be on her and Ben, not the decorations.

There were two tables on one end of the tent that would hold the food and beverages. After the ceremony, the wedding party and the guests would sit down to a delicious brunch. Available to eat would be a build-your-own waffle bar and a mixed fruit bar. There would also be flavored water, coffee, and different juices.

At the other end was a table decorated as a place for cards and gifts. This was also where a large picture frame was placed for guests to sign. The couple had decided that having a signed frame would be more meaningful than a guest book. They planned on hanging one of their wedding pictures in the frame and putting it in their entryway.

Shaya had printed several photos that were placed on various tables. She was happy that she had saved the photos from when they dated all those years ago. That added a fun touch.

Shaya's nerves were as rattled as they could be as she prepared to walk down the aisle. Her mother and Jexi were helping her slip into her wedding dress and Aunt Katie had done her hair. She couldn't understand what was causing her to be so nervous until the reality of what was happening hit her like a lightning bolt. She was about to be married to the love of her life. She would be moving out of the little apartment she shared with Jexi and into the house Ben had built for them. She wouldn't be a girlfriend or fiancée e anymore, she would be a wife.

While Attie was helping with Shaya's dress, Shaya looked at her reflection in the mirror. She noticed a tear running down her mother's cheek.

"Don't cry, Mama," Shaya said. "If you start, I might start too."

"I can't help it. My baby girl is getting married." Attie sniffled. "This is what mamas do."

The photographer recognized the beauty of the moment and continued to snap pictures of the exchange.

Shaya turned to hug her mom. "Love you, Mom," she said.

"I love you too, baby," replied Attie.

Shaya pulled away from her mother and looked at Jexi. "Are you okay?" she asked.

"Yeah," Jexi said. "Why wouldn't I be? It's not like I'm crying or anything." She quickly wiped away a tear.

Shaya rolled her eyes at her best friend. "I'm not a dummy, you know. I can clearly see when your mind is running full speed ahead. You aren't thinking about 'him' are you?"

"Don't be silly," Jexi retorted. "This day is all about you. Trust me, I'm okay. I promise!"

"Then why were you crying?" Shaya asked accusingly.

"Well, if you must know, I thought that moment between you and your mom was particularly touching," Jexi answered. "Plus, I'm super happy for you."

"Oh, okay," Shaya said. "I had to check. It's my job, and all."

Aunt Jessie rushed into the bedroom where the ladies were dressing. "Shay, your dad is here. He wants to see you before he walks you down the aisle."

Everybody scurried to make sure the final touches were completed. After a moment, Shaya took a deep breath. "Okay, let him in," she said.

Rance Clark walked into the room and stopped short when he saw his daughter, dressed as a bride, standing before him.

"Hi, Daddy," Shaya said, as she moved forward to hug him.

In a strangled voice, Rance replied. "Hi, sweet pea. You look stunning."

"Did you need something? You aren't backing out, are you?" Shaya asked.

"Oh heavens, NO. I just wanted to see you before the ceremony so I could get my tears out of the way," Rance choked out. "Nobody wants to see the bride's father blubbering like a baby."

Attie cleared her throat. "Hello, Rance," she said. "How are you?"

Rance wiped his tears and looked toward her. "Hi, Attie. You look good. It's been a while."

Aunt Katie practically knocked the door down when she rushed in and yelled, "SHOWTIME!"

Rance looked at Shaya. "Ready, kiddo?"

Shaya put her hand in the crook of her father's arm. "Ready, Dad," she responded.

Aunt Katie and Aunt Jessie rushed out to take their seats. Attie walked to greet her eldest son, who would walk her to her chair. The processional began and the ceremony started.

While the bridesmaids and groomsmen were walking down the aisle, Rance and Shaya stood waiting for their turn. Quietly, Rance whispered to his daughter, "Thank you for including me in your big day, hon. It means a lot to me."

"You're my dad. I wanted you to be here with me," Shaya whispered, and then added, "I love you, Daddy. Thanks for coming."

"I love you too, Shaya," answered her father.

The bridal song began to play, and Shaya knew it was her moment. She was excited and nervous at the same time. She and her father started down the aisle as the guests all stood. Shaya leaned toward her dad, "Please don't let me trip and fall."

Her dad grinned. "I've got you, darling. Always."

Shaya saw Ben toward the front and watched as he brushed a tear from his face. *Aww, he's crying,* Shaya noticed. When she and her father reached the end of the walk, Ben approached her. Pastor Dave looked at her father and asked, "Who gives this woman's hand in marriage?"

"Her mother and I do," responded Rance. He kissed his daughter on the cheek and went to sit next to Attie.

Ben and Shaya joined hands, and the pastor proceeded with the ceremony. Attie and her sisters cried throughout the whole wedding. While Ben and Shaya were braiding three cords together, Aunt Katie blew her nose loudly. This caused everyone to laugh and even Ben and Shaya giggled.

After the cords had been braided, Pastor Dave explained what the demonstration meant. "We show three strands braided together to represent the marriage bond with God in the center. It is modeled after Ecclesiastes four, nine through twelve. 'Two are better than one, because they have a good return for their labor: If either of them falls down, one can help the other up. But pity anyone who falls and has no one to help them up. Also, if two lie down together, they will keep warm. But how can one keep warm alone? Though one may be overpowered, two can defend themselves. A cord of three strands is not quickly broken.' This shows that when a couple has God at the center of their marriage, the two of them can face the storms of life."

Then Pastor Dave announced that the couple would be reading vows they had written themselves.

Ben reached into his coat pocket for a small piece of paper. "Shaya," he began, "I didn't have to think about my vows because I already know how I feel about you in my heart. You are my one and only." Ben paused to wipe a tear from Shaya's face. "I have loved you for so long and I can promise that I will love you for eternity. God gave you back to me for a second chance and I intend to honor and protect you for the rest of our lives. Our marriage will be centered in Christ and with Him as our guide."

Shaya was shaking as she began to read her vows to Ben. "Ben, I cannot deny how much I love you. I know, because I tried," Shaya smiled up at Ben as the crowd giggled. "I also promise to love you for eternity. I will support and honor you always. God will lead us through each day as we navigate these waters. You are the piece that has been missing in my life and I look forward to having you by my side for the rest of our days."

Sniffles and sounds of *"Aww"* came from the crowd. Aunt Katie blew her nose loudly again, resulting in more laughter.

Pastor Dave continued with the service. The rings were exchanged and then the pastor said, "Ben and Shaya, as you stand before God today, uniting as husband and wife, I ask that you always remember the vows you said. Be quick to forgive, as God forgives us. Comfort each other, as God comforts us. Cherish one another, as God cherishes his children. May your home be filled with grace, love, and mutual respect. It takes a lot of faith for a couple to start a new life together. Always keep God in the center of your family and trust Him to lead you." Pastor Dave paused and continued. "By the authority vested in me by the state of Kansas, I now pronounce you husband and wife." He looked at Ben, "You may kiss your bride."

Ben released Shaya's hands and moved his arms around her waist to pull her in for a deep kiss. Their guests erupted with loud cheers. Ben and Shaya turned toward the crowd and waved at everyone. Pastor Dave announced, "May I now present to you, Mr. and Mrs. Thatcher!"

The newlywed couple walked toward the back of the chairs and headed to the house for a private moment. They both had large smiles on their faces as they walked into the living room. Once they were alone, Ben kissed Shaya again. Ben asked her, "Are you ready to face everyone?"

Shaya nodded. "As ready as I'll ever be. I guess the hard part's over, huh?" She laughed as she nudged Ben with her elbow.

"Marrying me was difficult?" Ben asked with a pretend hurt in his voice.

"Not at all," Shaya answered him. "As a matter of fact, it was one of the easiest things I've ever done."

They walked out to the gazebo where the photographer was waiting to get more pictures. They only had a few images that they wanted to capture, and the session didn't take very long. They then set off to enjoy their reception.

The rest of the day went by quickly. Some family and friends helped move the gifts to the new house after the reception. The couple had plans to leave for their honeymoon after church the next day. That night, they were both fatigued from the day and fell asleep easily. Just before she dozed off, Shaya looked at the ring finger on her left hand where a beautiful diamond sat. I am *Mrs. Ben Thatcher,* she thought. *Mrs. Thatcher. I never dreamed that I could be this happy.*

CHAPTER EIGHT

It was strange for Jexi to wake up in the apartment, knowing that Shaya wasn't there and wouldn't be there anymore. It was kind of a lonely feeling, but she was happy for Shaya and wouldn't have it any other way. She hurried to get ready for church. She wanted to get there early enough to talk to the new Mrs. Thatcher before she and Ben left for their honeymoon.

She successfully found her best friend inside the church and the two shared quality time over morning coffee. The two sat together during the service, which was fantastic, as always. It seemed like church was Jexi's favorite place these days. She would miss it while she was in Honduras.

Sunday afternoon, Jexi was rearranging furniture and doing her best to make the small apartment less empty when her phone rang. She gently dropped the end of her sofa and looked at the caller ID. It was Jessie.

"Jexi, are you sitting down?" she asked.

"Yeah," Jexi replied. "What is wrong? You sound so upset!"

"It's Juan Carlos," Jessie began to explain. "I don't know how to say this other than to just come out and say it . . ." her voice faltered.

"Aunt Jessie!" Jexi snapped. "What is it?!"

"He's missing!" Jessie bellowed between sobs. "No one in the village has seen him for two days. There is no answer on his cell phone. He left Friday morning to pick up supplies in town and has not returned. He has never gone overnight before, without letting someone know. Please pray for them!"

"OH NO!" Jexi yelled. "And with Angelica being pregnant, I bet she is a mess right now. And the babies! Well, I'm glad we are leaving tomorrow! Maybe we can help."

"Child, I love your tenacity," said Jessie. "But what can we possibly do besides pray? I can't just let you go traipsing all over Honduras! It's completely unsafe!"

"But," argued Jexi, "there HAS to be something we can do other than just pray! Can we put up flyers or gather a search party? What about the police? Can we contact them?"

Jessie interrupted. "I know how much you care. But prayer isn't our last option, it's our best option. We activate the power of heaven when we pray. Honey, prayer is the strongest and should be the first action that we take. Besides, we are leaving tomorrow and will be there soon enough. We can be a good support for Angelica and the kids."

Jexi sighed. "I'd never thought of prayer like that."

"Get some rest tonight. You're going to need it," Jessie said. "You know what? How about you come to stay at my house tonight? That way you won't be alone letting your mind wander."

"Okay," Jexi agreed. "Let me pack the rest of my things and I'll be over. Thank you. I think you're right about me not being alone."

"Oh," Jessie started. "I forgot to tell you that we are riding to the airport with Hunter. It will be easier for him to pick us up in one place."

Jexi felt a shudder of excitement and she attempted to hide this from her voice. "Oh, okay," she said. "I guess that does make the most sense."

Jessie laughed. "Okay, child. See you in a little bit."

Jexi's alarm blared early Monday morning. She reached over and shut it off. She groaned at the early hour, but she was also giddy for the trip to come. She had been grateful for Jessie's invitation to stay over; she always found it so easy to talk to her. Jexi rolled out of bed and prepared for their journey. When she walked into the kitchen, Hunter was sitting at the table eating breakfast with Jessie.

"Good morning, Hun," Aunt Jessie said. "I invited Hunter to join us for breakfast. It's the least I could do since he offered to drive for us."

Jexi gulped. She hadn't expected him to be there this early. She was secretly glad she had taken a little extra time to put on her makeup.

"Hey there!" Hunter greeted. "Hope you don't mind that we started without you."

"Good morning, and not at all," Jexi returned. When she sat down at the table, Jessie began piling food on her plate before she could even say anything else. Jexi realized what she was doing and stopped her. "Aunt Jessie, thanks but that's enough. I don't want a big meal on my tummy for the flight."

Jessie looked offended. "Well, alright, I don't want to force anything on you that you don't want," she said with hurt in her voice. "I'm not your mama but I sure think you should eat a good meal."

Jexi giggled. "You sure know how to pull a guilt trip on someone! I'll take more, please."

Jessie's smile returned. "That's my girl!" she said as she plopped another helping of sausage on Jexi's plate.

Hunter laughed. "You'll learn soon enough that you don't refuse anyone's cooking around here. It's just easier to eat it with a smile and a thank you."

"Thank you, Aunt Jessie," Jexi said with a smile.

The three finished breakfast and washed up the dishes. Soon it was time for them to put all their luggage into Hunter's car and head to Kansas City. Aunt Jessie got into the backseat and started to buckle her seatbelt.

Jexi objected. "Aunt Jessie, you get in the front seat. I'll be fine in the back."

Jessie winked at her and giggled. "I might just want to tip my head back and rest a bit on the drive. This way, you and Hunter can easily chat with each other."

Jexi wanted to growl at her, but the truth was that she was excited to spend this time with Hunter. She climbed into the front and settled in for a long trip. She provided Hunter with the address to her parents' house so he could plug it into his GPS. Within a few minutes, they were on the road.

They drove in silence for the first fifteen minutes. Jexi could hear Jessie breathing deeply and knew she was asleep already. "It's a good thing we didn't let her drive," Jexi told Hunter.

Hunter laughed, "No kidding! She must not have gotten much sleep last night. She was telling me about some guy that is missing in the village. Do you know anything about that?"

Jexi sighed. "Yeah, she's talking about Juan Carlos. He went missing sometime on Friday. We are very scared for him. These people are so kind, Hunter, you're going to love them. We just have to find Juan Carlos! He and his wife Angelica have six children and another one on the way!"

"Wowza! That's a lot of kids," exclaimed Hunter. "I thought this place was poverty-ridden. How can they afford to care for that many children?"

"They trust God to meet their needs first of all," Jexi answered. "But they also grow the majority of their own food, and they only eat two large meals a day. Their lunch is usually very light. That helps the food to stretch longer. I've also seen some of the adults give up some of their food to help feed the younger children. It's so touching. They are some of the most loving and generous people I've ever met."

"Tell me about the kids," Hunter said.

"Juan Carlos, Junior is the oldest. He's about twenty-one and we call him JC or Junior. He is courting a young lady by the name of Maya. I expect they will soon be married. JC does a lot to help the family and the village. He's a really good kid. Angelica is not his biological mother. He and Carlita's mother died during childbirth when Carlita was born."

"That's too bad," Hunter interjected.

"Carlita is a beautiful young girl. She has caught the eye of many of the village boys," Jexi continued.

Hunter grinned, "Oh yeah?" he asked. "Beautiful, huh?"

Jexi rolled her eyes. "She's only eighteen, Casanova. Too young for you."

Hunter snickered. "I was kidding, you know."

"Besides, she has her eyes on Antonio Valdez. He lives in the village with his parents, Ricky and Barrialina. They are another wonderful family," Jexi smiled and added. "I could go on and on about these people."

"Go ahead," Hunter said. "We have three hours. Finish telling me about the kids first."

Jexi went on with her story. "Next is Diego. He's fourteen and Angelica's firstborn. He tries so hard to be a man and do the things his older brother does. He's just not quite as strong yet, so it's so cute. He loves to play soccer. When I was there last, he and I would watch soccer videos, and he would try to mimic the professionals.

"Then Dante, he's twelve. A lot of the time, he follows Diego all over the place. He loves nature. If he's not in the village, he's in the forest, looking at animals, bugs, and trees. It wouldn't surprise me if he became an entomologist or zoologist someday. It would be great if he gets a grant sponsorship to go to college. I know his family won't be able to afford to send him.

"Next comes Sophia who is nine. She is so precious. She loves music and loves to sing. It's surprising how good of a voice she has at such a young age. She is shy, though, and not very many people get to hear her. I got lucky one afternoon, and she didn't know I was near the schoolhouse. She was singing and it was so beautiful. I don't even know what the song was about because it was in Spanish, but it was still incredible! She loves to hear stories about the United States. She hopes to be a famous singer someday in the States.

"Lastly, there is Natalia. Don't tell the others, but she's my favorite. This girl made me cry tears of happiness. It was the most adorable moment. The kids don't know a whole lot of English and when she saw me tear up, she told me, 'No sad,' and wanted me to hold her. Her heart is fine-tuned to others' feelings, and she just seems to know when someone needs her. She is going to do great things one day. Maybe as a teacher or maybe as a nurse, or whatever, I don't know, but she will do great things."

Hunter smiled at Jexi. "You really love them. I can hear it when you talk about them. I've not heard you this passionate about anything before."

'I do," Jexi said. "I don't see how anyone can't love them once they get to know them. They are humble and loving and generous and so faithful. I have so much to learn from them! They don't have much, yet they have everything."

"I can't wait to meet them," Hunter said.

"I am thankful that you are coming to help with the well," Jexi said. "Plus, maybe you can help them find Juan Carlos."

Hunter shrugged. "I will do whatever I can to help," he said. "We will see what the situation is once we get there."

"I know God is in control," Jexi started, "but I can't help but be worried about him."

"Let me tell you a little something that I've learned about God," Hunter said. "He will work everything for His good. Whether we find Juan Carlos or not, God will use this situation for the good of His kingdom."

"What do you mean?" asked Jexi.

"There is a verse in Romans, I can't remember the exact chapter, but I'll summarize it. It says that we know God works all things for the good of those who love Him. That doesn't mean that everything that happens to us will be good, but it does mean that what happens will work out to glorify God. He finds a way to turn icky situations into something positive. You know the saying, if life gives you lemons, God turns it into a lemon-berry slush. So in applying it to Juan Carlos's absence, no matter what happens, we will be able to praise God."

"I have never heard that saying," Jexi said with a little laugh.

The car got quiet again and Jexi thought for a few moments about what Hunter said. She was concerned that Juan Carlos could be hurt, or even worse, but she was afraid to vocalize those thoughts. She wanted to believe in the best-case scenario.

Hunter spoke up. "I can see that you're really worried." He reached his right hand out and said, "Give me your hand."

Jexi looked at him quizzically. "Why?" she asked.

"Just do it," Hunter said. "Trust me."

Jexi extended her left hand and placed it in his. Hunter began to pray. "Father God, we are so grateful for You. Thank You that we can go to Honduras and be Your helping hands. God, we are worried about our friend, Juan Carlos. But we also know that You are in control, and You know exactly what will happen. We trust You and trust that You will cause everything to work into a lemon-berry slush. Keep Juan Carlos safe and bring him back to his village unharmed. Also, allow Your peace to fill Jexi and all those who love Juan Carlos. In Jesus' name, we pray, Amen."

Jexi was in awe. She had been taken aback when Hunter prayed; she wasn't expecting that. However, she was pleasantly surprised at the gesture. Immediately she felt a calm wash over her.

CHAPTER NINE

As soon as Ken and Sharon's van pulled into the village, Jexi jumped out. The villagers were all there waiting to greet them. Carlita ran to her and threw her arms around Jexi. As the girl sobbed on Jexi's shoulder, she whispered, "Thank you for coming."

Jexi felt a small body press against her legs and little arms wrapped around her waist. "Hi, Natalia. I missed you so much!" She reached down and picked the girl up and squeezed her tight.

Natalia whispered into Jexi's ear, "Who dat man?"

Jexi giggled, "This is Hunter. He came with us to help."

"Find daddy?" Natalia asked.

Hunter patted the little girl on the back and responded to her question. "We are going to do everything we can for your daddy."

Jessie looked around the villagers and noticed that Angelica was not with them. "Where is Angelica?" she asked one of the women.

"She no feel good now," the woman answered. "She rest."

Jessie nodded in understanding and started walking toward the home that Juan Carlos shared with her. She knocked on the door before opening it a crack. "Angelica?" she called. "May I come in?"

A faint yes emitted from the bedroom and Jessie walked in to sit by her bed. Angelica looked pale and weak but attempted to sit up when Jessie entered. "No, no, you lay down," Jessie implored. She could tell that Angelica had been crying and she realized that this was not healthy for the pregnancy. She tried to reassure her. "We are going to gather a search party," she said. "We will find him. Have you contacted the police?"

Angelica sniffled. "We try, but they say there is nothing they can do. He is grown man and can leave when he wants." She sighed. "But

I scare," she admitted. "This afternoon JC receive letter from mean people who say they have him." Angelica began to cry more.

"A letter?" Jessie inquired. "Where is it?"

"On the table," Angelica answered.

Jessie walked to the table and picked up the letter. She read it out loud. "We have your father, Juan Carlos. He is safe. If you want him to stay that way, you will convince the rest of the villagers to leave this land." Jessie looked at Angelica. "Is this from McGreggor?" she asked.

"Don't know," Angelica answered, "but we think."

Jessie scowled. "You stay here and rest. We will handle this. May I take this letter with me?"

Angelica nodded, *"Si,* I no move."

Jessi burst out of the hut and searched the crowd for Jexi and Hunter. She saw Hunter's tall frame in the mix and ran to him. "Hunter, grab Jexi. I need to talk to you guys. Hurry!" She moved back out of the circle and waited.

Hunter walked to Jexi and whispered in her ear. She immediately told the girls that she would be back in just a little while. She motioned to Ken and Sharon to join them, and they all walked over to Jessie.

"What's going on, Aunt Jessie?" Jexi asked.

"Angelica told me that JC got a letter today saying that there are people who have Juan Carlos! He's not missing, he's been kidnapped!"

Ken's mouth dropped open. "Kidnapped?!" he exclaimed. "What?"

Hunter also had a look of shock on his face. "Can I see the letter?" he asked.

Jessie handed it to him, and he read it aloud. "Yeah, he's been kidnapped, alright," he said. "We need to call the police right now!"

Ken put his hand on Hunter's shoulder. "I appreciate your enthusiasm, son, but the Honduran police won't be able to do much. They may not even want to get involved."

"It's worth a try!" Jexi pleaded. "How can the police not be able to help? They're the police, for crying out loud!"

Jessie relented. "Fine, we can take the note to the police," she said. "But we can't all go. I think it would be best if Ken and Hunter talk to them."

The group unanimously agreed. But before they left, Jessie took a picture of the letter with her phone in case something happened to it. She handed the letter back to Hunter as he and Ken got into the van to drive to the police station.

While the guys were gone, Jexi distracted herself by playing with the children. She was very upset about the latest development, but she had no idea about what she could do to help. Snuggling with Natalia and Sophia gave her something to do.

The men had been gone quite a while when Jessie began to assist with dinner preparation. Several of the ladies helped as well, but there was an uncomfortable silence as they completed the various tasks. Everyone was frightened and nobody knew what to say.

Jexi saw the van in the distance and began yelling to the others that the guys were coming back. Everyone gathered in the center of the village to greet them and to hear any news.

The van came to a stop and the men climbed out to a sea of eager faces. Many people looked to see if Juan Carlos would be exiting the vehicle also, but no other doors opened.

Sharon approached Ken. "What happened? What did they say? Are they searching for Juan Carlos? Why didn't they come back to the village with you?"

Ken slowly shook his head. "They took the letter and said they would investigate it. That's all we got from them."

"That's it?!" Jexi screamed. "They aren't even going to search for him? Aren't they going to dust the letter for fingerprints and DNA? Aren't they going to search for the typewriter the letter was typed on?"

"We don't know. All they told us was that they would investigate it. That's it," Hunter said.

"Then we have to find him," Jexi said with determination.

"How do you plan to do that, child?" Jessie asked. She wrapped her arm around Jexi's shoulder. "I know how much you want to help, but you can't go running around Honduras just calling his name. None of us even know where to start looking."

Hunter spoke up. "We could start with the letter. It is the biggest clue we have right now. We know he is being held somewhere."

"But we don't know where," Sharon answered. "And there is a lot of Honduran wildernesses that is so unsafe! Plus, we don't know who has him. We think that the letter is from McGreggor, but we have no proof."

"He is the only one who wants this land," Ken argued. "You're right, we don't have proof, but we can be fairly sure that he's behind this whole thing."

Jexi sucked in a breath. "Hold on, I'll be right back!" She ran into their hut and dug through her suitcase until she found a notebook and pen. She returned to the group and declared, "Okay, I'm ready."

"For what?" Hunter asked with a quizzical look on his face.

"We can't keep track of the clues if we don't write them down," Jexi explained. She began writing notes about the letter. "This way, we can come back to see what has transpired."

Jessie giggled. "You are a tenacious little thing, aren't you?" she asked. "Well, I suppose you have a point. I've watched enough true crime dramas to know that even the best detectives take notes."

"Exactly!" Jexi said.

"So, what is our next step?" Hunter asked.

"We can't confront McGreggor," Ken mentioned. "He will completely deny involvement. I'm sure there are enough layers of goons between him and Juan Carlos so he can't be tied to anything."

"Let's start with the land ownership contract," Jexi said. "If we can find solid documentation that Juan Carlos and his people own the land, McGreggor will have no choice but to leave them alone."

"Now you're thinking," Jessie stated. "We need to get that contract reviewed to see if there are any loopholes for McGreggor to jump through or if it is ironclad. Who should review it?"

"Hunter and I will go to the courthouse tomorrow," Ken said as he glanced at his watch. "They've closed by now. The contract should be on file there."

Jessie's eyes widened. "Juan Carlos has a certified copy here in his hut!" she remembered.

Sharon smiled. "Oh, what a relief!" she said.

"I will go talk with Angelica," Jessie said. "I'm sure she knows where it is located. In the meantime, it smells like dinner is ready.

CHAPTER TEN

After breakfast the next morning, Ken and Hunter set off for the courthouse with the copy of the land deed. As they were getting into the
van, Ken turned to Sharon. "Hon, don't forget, Jorge is coming today
to give us an estimate on the well drilling."

"Oh, I thought we were going to help dig the well," Hunter said.

"We may still do that, we are just getting a professional opinion
and determining if we can afford that route," Ken said.

"What time will Jorge arrive?" Sharon asked.

"Sometime before eleven," Ken said, as he put the van in gear and
drove away.

Jexi, Jessie, and Sharon helped clean up the breakfast dishes. Jexi
found herself anxious and unfocused with things she could do, but
nothing she wanted to do. She went to the hut and sat down on her
cot. She didn't like waiting. It made her uncomfortable. She wanted to
do something, anything, to help. She opened her notebook to the page
where she had written notes and reviewed the information they had so
far. This evil made no sense to her. This was not helping her anxiety.

She sighed as Jessie walked into the hut. "What's the matter, kid?"
Jessie asked.

Jexi looked up at Jessie. "I want to help. I want to find Juan Carlos.
I want to pack a backpack, get some water, grab a walking stick, and
head out to search for him. I want to call McGreggor and demand
that he releases him. I want to scream!" She took a breath and calmly
added, "I don't like just waiting."

Jessie smiled in her all-knowing way. "First of all, NO, you are
not going to head out as a one-person search party." She stopped and
softened her tone and sat down next to Jexi on the cot. "Sweetheart,

waiting is hard, isn't it?" she acknowledged. "But God is always in the waiting."

Jexi looked at her. "Yeah, yeah, I know," she mumbled.

"But I don't think you do," Jessie answered gently. "God's timing is perfect. He is never late and never early. He does everything at the exact right time."

Jexi snapped her head toward Jessie. "What are you talking about? This is far from perfect timing. Angelica is pregnant, and currently lying in her bed, sick. I don't see the perfection in that timing."

"God didn't cause Juan Carlos to be taken, but He did know it was going to happen," Jessie tried to explain. "He will use this for His glory. No matter what the outcome, God will bring good from it, and He will be praised. We just have to wait patiently on Him and pray for guidance."

"That's it?" Jexi asked skeptically.

"Yes," said Jessie. "Hold on a second." Jessie walked over to the nightstand next to her cot, picked up her Bible, and walked back to Jexi. She opened the book to Psalm, chapter thirty-seven, and started reading verse one. "Listen to this, 'Do not fret because of those who are evil or be envious of those who do wrong; for like the grass they will soon wither, like green plants, they will soon die away. Trust in the Lord and do good; dwell in the land and enjoy safe pasture. Take delight in the Lord and He will give you the desires of your heart. Commit your way to the Lord; trust in Him and He will do this: He will make your righteous reward shine like the dawn, your vindication like the noonday sun. Be still before the Lord and wait patiently for Him; do not fret when people succeed in their ways, when they carry out their wicked schemes. Refrain from anger and turn from wrath; do not fret—it leads only to evil.'" Jessie stopped at verse eight and looked at Jexi. "See, the Bible tells us to wait patiently." Jexi hung her head. "Okay," she conceded. "It's just really hard not to be angry. I guess I could use this time of waiting to do some Bible reading of my own."

"That's my girl," Jessie said. "Do you want me to stay with you?"

"If you don't mind," Jexi answered. "It's a little easier when I'm not alone."

Jessie sat back down next to Jexi and hugged her. "I feel the same way. It's always nicer to endure hard times with a friend."

Jexi smiled. "Tell me where you found that passage again, please?"

Jessie held out her Bible. "Psalm thirty-seven, verses one through eight."

The two sat in silence as they read their Bibles and soaked in the Lord's goodness. Jexi felt her body relax and her mind clear as she read the Word. She remembered this feeling of peace and thanked God for His goodness.

The next thing they heard was Sharon calling for them. "Jessie, Jexi, the well man is here!"

They exited the hut and went to the center area of the village to meet Jorge. After the introductions were complete, they led Jorge to the area where they had attempted to build the well.

Jorge walked around quietly for a moment as he surveyed the site. They heard him say *"Hmm"* a few times as he walked. "You picked a good spot. You are close to a water source, so that helps. You also have a good start to a well. However, you won't be able to go any deeper with human hands. You are going to need some specialized tools."

"Specialized tools?" Sharon asked. "What kind of tools? And how expensive will it be?"

"I have a well-digging kit at my shop as well as all of the extra tools you will need," Jorge answered. "I will loan you my air compressor and sell you the entire kit for nine hundred American dollars. And if you want me to do the work for you, it will cost another hundred."

"A thousand dollars?" JC asked with panic in his voice. "We no have that much money. Can you help us by making cheaper?"

Jorge shook his head. "Sadly, no. That is the cheapest I can go. I would barely make any profit as it is. You can look into other companies, but they will charge you much more, I guarantee."

Jexi grinned. "We'll do it!" she said with confidence.

JC and Carlita looked at her in disbelief. "We cannot!" Carlita exclaimed. "Did you no hear JC? We no have money!"

"But we do!" Jexi answered. "Remember, Aunt Jessie?! That stranger from Kansas City, Missouri, will pay for the well!"

Sharon was baffled. "Stranger from Kansas City?" she asked.

Jexi explained. "When we were home before our first trip here, a man handed us a check for a thousand dollars saying that we would need it for our second trip! I didn't even know we were going to be coming back at that time, but God knew! We thought we were going to need it for travel expenses, but we got enough donations from the church that we haven't spent that money yet."

Jessie threw her hands in the air. "Praise the Lord!" she yelled. "Sharon, she's right. Let's have Jorge dig the well professionally. Then the village can have fresh water a lot sooner and everyone will be safe! Plus, that will give us more time to help find Juan Carlos!"

Sharon looked at Jorge. "You heard the ladies! Let's build that well!"

Carlita rushed over to Jexi and hugged her with tears in her eyes. "Gracias, senorita," she said. *"Eres una benediction de Dios!* Thank you, you are a blessing from God."

JC had also walked over to her and wrapped his arms around Jexi and Carlita. *"Si,* gracias," he echoed.

Jexi laughed. "Don't thank me. Thank God and the random guy in Kansas City."

"Gracias, *Dios!"* JC said. "And a guy in Kansas City."

Sharon was crying as she watched the interaction. "God is so good!" she said. She turned to run. "I need to tell Angelica. This will ease some of her stress!"

Jessie turned to Jorge. "When will you get started?" she asked. "I can have the money for you tomorrow."

Jorge said, "I will come tomorrow and start early. Seven o'clock. Are there strong young men in the village willing to help?"

JC nodded. "Yes, there are many. We will help."

Jorge shook hands with JC and Jessie. "See you tomorrow morning then." He walked to his truck.

By the time Jorge's truck was gone, the news had spread through the entire village, and everyone was cheering. Sharon said that when she told Angelica, the baby leaped for joy in her womb. Yet as happy as they all were about the excitement, the worry about Juan Carlos still lingered in the air.

Within a few minutes, Ken and Hunter returned to Aldea Gracia. Jessie, Jexi, Sharon, JC, and Carlita rushed to tell them the good news. They were all talking at once because they were so enthusiastic.

"Whoa!" Ken hollered. "One at a time, please! We cannot understand a single one of you!"

JC stepped forward. "The man for the well came. He want one thousand dollars to build the well. At first we panic because we no have that money. But Jexi say that *el* hombre in Kansas City give us money to build the well and it will be done mañana!"

"What man from Kansas City?" asked Hunter.

"I'll explain later," Jexi replied.

Hunter and Ken both hollered whoops of joy. "That's great!" said Hunter.

Jessie pushed her way to Ken and Hunter. "What did you find out at the courthouse?" she asked.

"Nothing good," replied Ken. "They agree that the copy of the land deed looks legit, but they don't have the original document on file."

"How can they not have it?" Jexi asked. "They have to have it. That's their job."

Jessie put her hand on Jexi's arm to calm her. "What is the next step?" Jessie asked.

Hunter answered, "They promised us that they would look for it and let us know."

Jexi grunted in exasperation. "So, nothing, basically."

Jessie's hand squeezed Jexi's hand gently. "Don't forget our talk earlier," she reminded.

Jexi sighed. "You're right, I know," she mumbled.

Ken stepped to the middle of the throng. "We need to pray," he announced. Everyone stopped talking and bowed their heads. Ken continued, "Abba Father, we praise You. We are scared and worried, but we know that You are in control. We seek Your peace and ask that You please bring our brother Juan Carlos home to us. Please give us guidance on how to settle the land dispute. We ask that Your will be done, on earth, as it is in heaven. In Jesus' name, we pray. Amen."

While Ken prayed, Angelica cautiously and quietly made her way to the group. After his amen, she added in a soft voice, "Lord, we lift up Juan Carlos's kidnappers and ask You show them Your love and mercy. In Jesus' name, amen."

CHAPTER ELEVEN

Everyone turned to look at Angelica with surprise.

Anita walked to her. *"Miha,* why you pray for the bad men?"

Angelica took her mother-in-law's hands. "They need Jesus too, Mama," she answered. "We are to pray for our enemies, remember? We want them to treat Juan Carlos with kindness, *si?* We want them to know the love of God."

Anita lowered her head. *"Si, si,* we do want these things. I just so worry about my boy."

Angelica hugged her. "He is going to come home to us."

Jessie took Angelica by the hand. "You need to be in bed. Go lie down and I'll bring you something to eat."

"Si. Gracias," Angelica responded.

The group dispersed to their individual huts. As night fell upon the village, Jessie and Jexi prayed together. Jexi was in awe at how she had seen God work over the last several months. She wasn't sure how He would work this for His good, but she knew in her heart that He would.

Jorge arrived bright and early the next morning. He and the men of the village were primed to get started on the well. Hunter eagerly joined them. Hopefully, they would have it finished by the end of the day and be able to pull fresh, clean water from the earth.

Jexi took a few moments after breakfast to send Shaya a message. She hadn't wanted to interrupt her and Ben's honeymoon, but Shaya had insisted upon updates. "Hi! Hope you guys are having a wonderful honeymoon. I hate to bother you on your trip but since you said to update you, I have bad news. Juan Carlos has been kidnapped, and we don't know where to look for him. The police have not been helpful.

Please pray. The good news: We are getting the well dug today. I can't wait to tell you how God worked on that! Miss you!"

After she sent the text to Shaya, she set out for the schoolhouse. When she had some free time, she had been helping the children of the village learn more English. Even though she wasn't a licensed teacher, the kids were enjoying the lessons. It was just what Jexi needed to distract her from the situation at hand.

Within an hour, her phone rang. She asked the children to wait for a minute and walked outside to answer. "Hey, Shay!" she said. "You didn't need to call."

"Kidnapped?!" Shaya yelled into the phone. "When did this happen?" Jexi winced from the loud voice in her ear. "Well, he's been gone since Friday, so we are guessing that's when he was taken."

"And why didn't you say something sooner?!" Shaya yelled. "Who is your contact person for the mission work?"

"Ken and Sharon," Jexi replied.

"Are they there?" Shaya asked.

"Yes, they're here," answered Jexi. "Why? There isn't anything they can do either—"

Shaya cut her off. "May I please talk to one of them?" she asked.

"Uh, sure," Jexi said inquisitively and walked toward Sharon. "But why do you want to talk to them?"

"I'll tell you after I talk to one of them," Shaya responded.

Jexi tapped Sharon on the arm. "Excuse me, Sharon. My friend, Shaya, would like to talk with you. Do you have a minute?" she whispered to her.

Sharon gave Jexi a puzzled look. "Sure."

Jexi shrugged to Sharon and handed her the phone. "Her name is Shaya. I have no idea what she wants."

Sharon and Shaya talked for a couple of minutes while Jexi waited impatiently. Jexi heard Sharon talking to Shaya about the airport in Tegucigalpa. Then Sharon handed the phone back to Jexi. "Here ya go," she said. "You have a really special friend." She winked and then walked away.

"What in the thunder is going on?" Jexi asked.

"Ben and I are coming to Aldea Gracia," Shaya stated matter-of-factly.

"Did you even talk to Ben about this?" Jexi asked.

"I talked to him when I got your text and you've been on speaker. It was actually his idea," Shaya said.

Jexi began to cry. "You guys," she said. "That's so kind! But realistically, there isn't anything we can do. They won't let me go on a searching expedition and all we are doing is waiting."

"That's where you are wrong, bestie," Shaya said. "I have a friend who is a private investigator. I am going to call her and see if we can get her on a flight too. I know you love these people, and we can't let you go through this alone. I don't know if we can help find him, but we can for sure be supportive."

"I never knew that you knew a private investigator! That's so cool! It's just like Nancy Drew!" Jexi said. "So, you'll be here next week?"

"No, we'll be there as soon as we can get a flight out," Shaya answered.

"Don't cut your honeymoon short!" Jexi protested.

"You can't tell me what to do," Shaya retorted. "Besides, Ben and I already discussed it and he's already looking into airfare. I'll let you know what we figure out. Sharon already agreed to pick us up in Teg-Goosey-Goosey."

Jexi began to laugh uncontrollably. Between sputters she said, *"Teg-Goosey-Goosey?"*

"You know what I mean," Shaya said. "It's a hard name to remember and pronounce!"

"Tegucigalpa," said Ben, snickering. "Not that difficult."

Shaya yelled at him, "Shh!" and then began talking to Jexi again. "Okay, once we have all the details secured, we will text you. See you soon!"

She couldn't believe that Shaya and Ben were coming to Honduras. She also couldn't believe that Shaya knew a private investigator. She ran to the site of the well to find Jessie and Hunter. She excitedly informed them about Shaya and Ben coming to help and the news of them hiring a private investigator.

"Why did you interrupt their honeymoon?" Hunter asked.

"Because Shaya asked me to keep her in the loop," Jexi said defensively.

"So, are they coming next week after they return from their honeymoon?" Ben asked. "We may have Juan Carlos back by then."

"No! They are coming as soon as they are able," Jexi answered.

Jessie asked, "Where are they going to find a PI who will travel to Honduras to help? That's a lot to ask of a PI, and that will probably be expensive."

"I guess Shaya has a friend from college who studied criminal justice and then became a PI and this friend might be willing to take the case," Jexi explained.

"That is generous of them to cut their honeymoon short," said Hunter. "They are good peeps. I'm going to get back to working on the well. See ya."

Back in the United States, Shaya immediately pulled up the phone number for her friend, Harli Chase, and pressed the call button.

"Harli Chase, private eye, how can I help you?" Harli answered.

"Hi, Harli, this is Shaya . . . it's been a while," Shaya started.

"Shaya, I know it's you! My phone shows your name and picture. How are you? What's going on?" Harli asked.

"A lot, actually, and I'd love to spend some time catching up, but I have a more pressing issue to talk about first," Shaya said. "We need your professional help."

"Of course!" replied Harli. "What do you need?"

"Do you help in cases of kidnapping?" Shaya asked. "And do you have a passport?"

"Yes, I do," Harli answered. "And I wouldn't be much of a private eye if I didn't have a passport. I'm always jetting off here and there. Where are you at?"

"Well, my husband, Ben, and I are in the States, but headed to Honduras," Shaya informed her.

"Husband?! Ben?!" Harli exclaimed. "You're right, we do have a lot to catch up on! But I understand there are more urgent things to do first. Where in Honduras? And when will you need my services?"

"I promise that I will fill you in on everything. But for now, Tegucigalpa Airport, and then we get picked up to go to a little village called Aldea Gracia," said Shaya. "We need you as soon as possible if you can. A very special friend has been kidnapped, and we need to get him home safely."

"I've got a couple of other cases to hand off to some colleagues, but I can get to Honduras within the next day or two." Harli said, and then added, "I know we are friends, but I don't work for free."

"Completely understandable," Shaya replied. "What is your fee?"

"We can discuss that later on," Harli said. "Let's just get started. I need as many specifics as you can give me. This man's name, when and where he was last seen, suspects, family members, and unusual circumstances."

"I don't know everything," Shaya said. "I can tell you his name is Juan Carlos. I can give you the number of my best friend who has all the info you need."

"Please do," Harli said. "I'd like to talk to her straight away."

While Shaya gave Harli the information she needed, Ben was on his laptop making travel arrangements. When she hung up, Ben said, "I'm going to go to the front desk and let them know we are leaving earlier than expected. Perhaps they will refund the rest of our week."

Shaya asked, "When are we leaving?"

"I got us a flight leaving tomorrow morning. There was one flying out today at three, but I didn't think it would be too safe driving through sketchy areas after dark."

"Smart thinking," Shaya said. "Where is the itinerary? While you are gone, I will text the details to Jexi and Harli."

"It's open on my laptop," Ben replied. He grabbed the room key and headed to the lobby.

Shaya walked to the laptop and looked at the itinerary. She started typing it into her phone but stopped abruptly. "Oh Lord, I'm so sorry. We have been acting out of fear and impulse. We completely forgot to stop and pray about what You wanted us to do. Forgive us for our fumble. God, You are in complete control. We want to do Your will. Before I send this text, please guide me. If there is a better way, please show me. I pray this in Jesus' mighty name, amen."

Shaya's phone buzzed in her hand. She looked down at it and smiled. "Got my schedule clear and my flight booked. I'll be in Honduras tomorrow by noon," was Harli's text.

Shaya smiled. "Okay then. I guess it's a go!" She pressed send on her itinerary text.

Back in Honduras, Jexi was also praying. "God, thank You for giving me such faithful and loving friends. I want to learn to seek You first before all else. I pray that Juan Carlos is returned home safe and unharmed. However, over everything, God, I pray that Your will be done. I do not know what Your outcome will be, but I do know that it will be good. I place my trust in You, Lord. In Jesus' name, amen."

Immediately her phone chimed. She pulled up the texting app and saw a text from someone she didn't know. "Hello, my name is Harli Chase. I am a private investigator and a friend of Shaya. She gave me your phone number. I have agreed to take the case, and I will be in Honduras tomorrow to help."

CHAPTER TWELVE

The bulky man paced back and forth in front of the bars that caged Juan Carlos in the dungeon cell.

"You seem uptight, amigo," Juan Carlos said softly.

"I am not your friend," the man snapped with a snarl. "Be quiet, *silencio!"*

"What's your name?" Juan Carlos asked.

"Why do you care?" his guard quipped. *"Silencio!* Leave me alone."

Juan Carlos folded his hands together and began to pray aloud, using the Spanish language to say: "Father God, You are the Almighty. I am lifting this man to You and asking that You help him with whatever is bothering him."

"Shut UP!" the man yelled. "Why won't you just be quiet? I did not ask you to pray for me!"

Juan Carlos continued, "Give him Your peace and show him how much You care for him. In Jesus' name, amen."

The man stopped and stared at Juan Carlos. "Why did you pray for me?" he asked. "You are *muy loco.* You don't even know me."

"I do not have to know you," Juan Carlos said gently. "I know that God loves you and you are His child. That is all I need."

"Andre," the man said as he continued his pacing.

"My name is Juan Carlos. What bothers you, Andre?" asked Juan Carlos.

"Nothing," Andre replied. "I am only doing my job."

"Your soul seems unsettled," said Juan Carlos. *"¿Eres infeliz?* Unhappy?"

Andre did not respond. He just walked back and forth, back and forth. Juan Carlos began to sing. *"Dios, bueno es. Dios, bueno es. Dios, bueno es. Bueno es, El Senor."*

"Muy loco," Andre said. "It was nice of you, but Dios has never helped me. I don't want to hear about it. Can't you just be quiet?"

Juan Carlos paused. "Am I not allowed to praise my God even when being held captive?" he asked Andre. "I do not mean to bother you. But I do want to praise my God."

"Why would you?" Andre asked. "Do you not realize you are a prisoner with no freedom? Yet you think your God is so good."

"Some very nice people came to my village and taught me about a man named Paul who was also held with no freedom," Juan Carlos said. "Paul praised Dios, and the prison walls fell to the ground."

"I don't see the walls falling," Andre said with a chuckle. "It's not working."

"Not yet," Juan Carlos said with conviction. "Do you have a Bible?"

Andre rolled his eyes. "That is just an old story of a nice man. Nothing more. Just lay down."

Juan Carlos persisted. "I will lay down if you can find a Bible for me."

"Fine," Andre agreed. "I will see what I can do." "Gracias," replied Juan Carlos. "God will show His favor on you." Juan Carlos went back to singing, *"Dios, bueno es. Dios, bueno es. Dios, bueno es. Bueno es, El Senor."*

Andre continued pacing, doing his best to ignore Juan Carlos. He was in no mood for this today.

The afternoon progressed and, eventually, Andre walked out of the dark cellar area. He returned a short time later with dinner and a Bible for Juan Carlos. He slid both through the bars of the door. "Here you go," he said gruffly. "Now, quit pestering me, okay?"

"Gracias, again," said Juan Carlos. He bowed his head and prayed, "Lord, thank You for this wonderful meal. Bless the person who prepared it and Andre for delivering it. May the meal provide me with the strength and nourishment to keep praising You. Please watch over my family and keep them safe. You are all we need, Dios. We love You. In the name of Your Son, Jesus, amen." He looked at his plate and smiled. There wasn't much food, but he was thankful nonetheless. When he finished the meager scraps given to him, he asked Andre, "Would you like to hear a story?"

"How can you be so . . . so . . . thankful?" Andre asked. "You were given scraps. You are caged in a dungeon. Yet, you are so thankful. And now you ask if I want to hear a story like I am a little boy and as if your surroundings do not matter. I do not understand you."

"I am thankful for all that my God has given me," Juan Carlos answered. "If I were not caged here, I would not have met you, *mi amigo*. And now that I have this Bible, I can tell you a story. Would you like to hear it?"

"I do not want to hear your fairy tales," Andre answered. "We are not friends. You cannot be friends with someone who is keeping you in a cage. I am glad that I will be going home soon, and I won't have to listen to you anymore."

"Okay then. Another time," Juan Carlos said. He opened his Bible and read, "John three, sixteen. 'For God so loved the world, that He gave His one and only Son, that whoever believes in Him shall not perish but have eternal life.'"

Andre huffed and looked at his watch. As if on cue, his replacement walked through the door. Juan Carlos could hear Andre whispering to him. "This man is *loco*. Do not listen to him."

Juan Carlos grinned and settled into some hay on the floor for the night. "Goodnight, Andre!" he yelled. He looked forward to talking with Andre the next day and prayed for him as he fell asleep.

In the morning, Andre arrived after Juan Carlos had been up for quite a while. He was perplexed as Juan Carlos greeted him with a smile. *"Buenos dias,* Andre!" he said, cheerfully.

"Do not start with me today, old man," Andre said. "I just do not want to deal with your *disparates;* nonsense. Just leave me alone."

Juan Carlos was quiet as Andre had asked. He needed to wait for the right moment to show him God's love. He knew that this man was lost and needed to be shown the way. But he also knew that if he pushed too hard, he would turn Andre away and miss the opportunity. He prayed silently to God to show him when and what to say. In the waiting, Juan Carlos prayed and praised quietly, while Andre watched and listened.

That evening in Aldea Gracia, Ken was leading a Bible study for the villagers in the building used as a church and a schoolhouse. He was teaching on faith and began by quoting Romans five, verses one through five. "Therefore, since we have been justified through faith, we have peace with God through our Lord Jesus Christ, through whom we have gained access by faith into this grace in which we now stand. And we boast in the hope of the glory of God. Not only so, but we also glory in our sufferings, because we know that suffering produces perseverance; perseverance, character; and character, hope. And hope does not put us to shame, because God's love has been poured out into our hearts through the Holy Spirit, who has been given to us." He paused and looked at the group.

Jexi thought about Juan Carlos and the perseverance, character, and hope that he must be developing right now. She still worried about him, though.

Ken continued, "It's difficult to maintain our faith in trying times like these, but God promises to be with us. God never promised that life would be easy, but we do know that He will always be by our side. Listen to Romans chapter eight, verses thirty-eight and thirty-nine. 'For I am convinced that neither death nor life, neither angels nor demons, neither the present nor the future, nor any powers, neither height nor depth, nor anything else in all creation, will be able to separate us from the love of God that is in Christ Jesus our Lord.'

God is with each and every one of us right now and He is also with Juan Carlos.

"In Isaiah fifty-four, seventeen, the Bible tells us that 'no weapon forged against you will prevail, and you will refute every tongue that accuses you. This is the heritage of the servants of the Lord, and this is their vindication from me, declares the Lord.' We have His promise that our enemies will not prevail. We have to keep our faith strong and believe that Juan Carlos will return to us, unharmed."

After the prayer, Hunter found Jexi sitting by herself with tears in her eyes. He sat next to her and gently touched her shoulder. "Did you hear what Ken said?" he asked. "We have to keep our faith strong. Juan Carlos will be okay."

"I know," Jexi said with a sniffle. "I'm just so scared for him and his family. What if . . . ."

Hunter embraced her with a hug. "Stop," he said quietly. "Trust God."

Jexi rested her head on Hunter's shoulder. "Thank you for being here for the villagers." She paused. "And for me."

Hunter leaned his head over hers. "Of course," he replied. "You are important to me."

Jexi looked up at him. His words were unexpected and yet comforting at the same time. She realized, in that instant, that Hunter was important to her too.

"Don't look so shocked," Hunter said. "Get to bed. Tomorrow will be a big day." He squeezed her shoulder and then stood up. Jexi watched as he walked out of the room. That familiar feeling of calm and peace washed over her once again and she relished the moment.

CHAPTER THIRTEEN

Thursday evening, Jexi watched with excitement as Ken and Sharon's van pulled into Aldea Gracia. She couldn't wait to hug her best friend and meet Harli in person. She had been texting Harli with details of Juan Carlos's kidnapping so that she would be up to speed when she arrived in Honduras. Something about Harli caused Jexi to like her instantly.

As she stood there, she felt a warm presence behind her. She turned to see Hunter standing there. "Are you excited too?" he asked.

"Oh, yes!" Jexi replied. "I've really missed her."

The moment the van stopped, and Shaya opened the door, Jexi ran and snatched her up into a giant bear hug. "I'm so glad you are here!"

Shaya hugged her back and laughed. "Easy!" she said. "Don't choke me!"

Jexi teared up. "I didn't know how much I needed you."

Shaya laughed. "Don't make it weird."

"Too late!" Jexi said as she pulled away.

Hunter and Ben shook hands and hugged. "I'm happy to see you, brother," Hunter said. "You didn't have to cut your honeymoon short just to come here, though."

"We're happy to help," Ben replied. "I knew as soon as Shaya heard about the trouble here, she would want to come. Plus, God let us both know that He wanted us to be here."

Jexi looked over Shaya's shoulder and saw a tiny little woman, with a long, blonde ponytail, stepping out of the van. "You must be Harli," she said.

"Nice to meet you," Harli said as she reached out to shake hands with Jexi.

Jexi bypassed her hand and hugged her instead. "You get more than a handshake for being here. Thanks for helping us," Jexi said.

Shaya felt a hand on her shoulder, and she turned around to see Aunt Jessie. The two embraced and Jessie expressed her gratitude toward her also. "Aunt Jessie, did you really think that I'd hear about something like this and not want to help?" she asked.

Jessie laughed, "I know how determined you are, that's for sure! You get it from your mother."

Shaya tapped her aunt on the shoulder in a fake slap. "AND my aunt."

Sharon stepped over to the group. "Let's get the luggage unloaded and taken to the huts." She opened the back of the van, and the men came around the side to gather the suitcases.

"I thought you guys would have more stuff since you came straight from your honeymoon," Hunter said.

Ben laughed. "We would have, but we shipped some of our things home before we left."

"What a good idea!" Jexi said. "I don't think I would have thought to do that."

"It was Ben's idea," Shaya added. "He's handsome AND smart." Shaya leaned in to kiss her new husband.

"I hope you guys don't mind splitting up," Aunt Jessie said. "There aren't enough huts for a newly married couple to have privacy." She winked. "We have a bunk for the men and a bunk for the women."

Ben bumped shoulders with Hunter. "This should be fun!"

Harli approached Jexi. "I'd like to go over the information you've sent me and see if you have anything you'd like to add. My goal is to get an early start in the morning."

"You got it," Jexi said. "Let's put our stuff in the huts and tell the others."

"That's great," Harli answered. "Is there somewhere we can meet?"

"Yeah, we can meet at the schoolhouse," Jexi said, pointing in the correct direction.

Jexi walked ahead to inform Ken, Hunter, and Ben, who were walking toward their hut, that Harli wanted to meet with them. She then went to her hut and realized that Harli had already told Jessie and Shaya. Jexi dug out her notebook and pen and the group walked to the schoolhouse.

Harli addressed them as they entered. "I have gotten a lot of details from Jexi, but I want to make sure I have absolutely everything. Any small memory might help, so don't be afraid to share it, even if you think it's insignificant."

"Should we get JC and Angelica?" Sharon asked.

"No, Angelica is too weak and in no shape for this," Jexi protested.

"I am just fine," Angelica said as she walked in to sit down.

"Oh, Angelica!" Jexi exclaimed. "I'm sorry. You have been so sick lately. I just want to protect you."

"*Gracias,* senorita," Angelica said. "But this is my love who is missing." She began to tear up but quickly regained her composure.

JC stepped into the room with Carlita. "She's stubborn," JC said. "But we all want to help too."

Harli smiled. "I know you do. And it is good that you are all here. You must be his children."

JC answered. "*Si,* I am Juan Carlos, Junior, but they call me JC." He pointed to his sister. "This is Carlita, my sister. The other children are too young to attend."

"I understand," said Harli. "But, at some point, I would like to just talk with them. You'd be surprised at how much little children know." She paused and looked around the room before bringing her focus back to Angelica. "What can you tell me about the day of his disappearance?" She looked at Jexi. "Will you take some notes for me in your notebook?" Jexi nodded with enthusiasm.

Angelica took a deep breath. "It was just like every other day when he takes things to the city. We had breakfast as a family and then Juan Carlos loaded the cart with crops."

Harli interrupted. "I'm sorry. I'm new here. Can you tell me why he was taking things to the city?"

Jessie answered. "Juan Carlos and the rest of the villagers grow a lot of crops in this area. They sell some of the crops to stores in the city so that they have the money to buy items that they are unable to make or produce themselves."

Harli pondered that information. "Who does he sell to? Is it always the same person or is it more? I'll want that information so I can ask questions. Do you know how to contact the buyers?"

JC spoke next. "He takes crops to Choluteca and sells to three stores there. He goes two times every month. I can give you the names of the shop owners. I go with him on many trips. I can go with you if you want."

"How come you didn't go with him this time?" Harli asked him.

"I was helping dig the well," JC answered. "He worry that the village would need more protection, so he ask me to stay back."

Harli furrowed her brow. "Protection?" she asked. "From who? Do you think those are the same people who sent the letter that you received on Monday?"

"Oh, I am sure of it," replied Ken. "Mr. McGreggor is a bad man. He has pushed other villages nearby to leave their land. He has been trying to get them to leave for three months, but they won't leave. Juan Carlos refused his offer many times."

"My Papa wants us to stay here," JC said. "He knows that Mr. Henderson made it legal for us to stay. We love this land, and our family has been here for many generations."

"Jexi told me about the contract," Harli said. "I know Ken and Hunter said the courthouse doesn't have the original, but I plan on talking with them later." She paused to gather her thoughts. "Okay, so let me make sure I have this straight. You've been getting letters telling you all to leave. Then Juan Carlos goes missing and you get a ransom letter telling you to convince everyone to move away if you want to get him back. Have you had any other interaction or contact with McGreggor?"

"Well," JC started. "We think so."

"You think so?" Harli asked. "Explain."

"The trucks," said Angelica. "They drive around the village with men in the back holding guns. They do not stop, and they do not say anything, but they are there."

Harli looked at her alarmed. "How often?" she asked.

"Once a week or something like that," JC answered.

The fear in Jexi's heart was growing. She knew of the one truck they had seen a while back, but she was not aware that there were trucks coming out at least once a week. *These people must be living in constant fear,* she thought. *God, please protect them!*

"It's obvious that this McGreggor guy has Juan Carlos," Shaya interjected.

"We can deduce that quite easily," Harli said, "But I guarantee you that he will deny any knowledge of anything. There are most likely multiple people between him and Juan Carlos so it cannot be traced back to him. We have to go about this very carefully so that we can substantiate his involvement." She looked back to JC. "Do you know why he wants you to leave your village?"

JC shook his head. "No, he has never told us," he said. "He has a lot of money. We don't know his job or what he would want with our little piece of land."

Jexi scoffed. "He has like a thousand acres of land. Why would he want these few acres?"

Harli shrugged. "We don't know, but we know that, legally, Aldea Gracia is safe. We just need to prove it."

The room was quiet as everyone processed the information. Hunter broke the silence. "Where do we start? I mean . . . what's our next step?"

Harli looked at him. "I want to talk with the children before they go to bed tonight. Tomorrow morning, I will start with the courthouse.

Finding that contract will be crucial in this process, and we will need it. Who has your copy?"

Angelica spoke softly. "It is at our home," she said. "Ken and Sharon kindly gave us a safe and we have placed it in there."

"May I borrow it?" Harli asked. Angelica nodded in response. "I will go with Angelica to her home to get the contract and see the children. That's all we can do tonight. Everyone, get some rest. I will update everyone tomorrow."

"What time are we leaving?" JC asked.

Harli answered. "Maybe around eight o'clock? It is best for only one or two of us to go to the courthouse. It could be seen as a threat if many of us go. JC, you will go with me, and you can also show me the stores that your father sells crops to. I will interview the owners to see what information I can gather from them." She started to walk to the door but then abruptly stopped. "What was Juan Carlos driving? Have they located that vehicle yet?"

"He was driving an old green Dodge truck, with wooden slats on the bedside," Ken answered. "When we spoke with the police, we were told that no one had found it yet."

"Interesting," Harli said. "One more thing. Can the police be trusted?" The room was silent. "Okay, I'll take that as a no."

CHAPTER FOURTEEN

The next morning, JC and Harli set off to the courthouse. JC was able to provide a few more details for Harli on the way. Harli had talked with the younger children the night before but had not gained any new knowledge about Juan Carlos's disappearance.

"You ask for the document first," Harli told JC. "They are more likely to trust you. I'll jump in when I feel it's necessary."

They entered and got in the appropriate line to wait their turn. Soon, they approached the window. "Hola," JC said. He pulled out the only copy of the contract. "I would like to see the original of this document *por favor.*"

The clerk reviewed the paper and handed it back to JC and held up one finger in a waiting gesture. *"Un momento,"* she said. She left the window and walked to a file cabinet and began looking. She pulled out a file folder and returned to the window. "There is nothing," she said as she held up the empty folder.

JC began to ball up his fists, but Harli gently touched his shoulder to help him calm down. "May we see the manager?" Harli asked.

The clerk looked confused. JC clarified, *"Supervisor,"* he added in Spanish. A look of understanding came over the clerk's face and she walked into a different room.

Harli noticed that the clerk at the next window was glancing at them and listening to their conversation. He was attempting to make himself look inconspicuous, but Harli was trained to recognize body language. Harli walked to him and nodded. "Hola," she said. "What do you know about this?"

"Nada, nothing, senora," the clerk answered. "Two men came before asking about the paper, and I talk to them. That is all I know." The man busied himself with the papers in his hand.

Harli's gut told her that this man knew more than he was admitting. She looked at the nameplate sitting on the counter and read it to herself. *Manuel Escobar. He knows something,* she thought. She took a business card and slid it to him on the counter. "If you can remember anything that might help, please contact me."

The supervisor returned at that moment and saw Harli talking with Manuel. She quickly hurried back to where JC was standing. "We do not have this document," the supervisor stated. "We have looked, but it is not here. Your document looks valid with our court stamp but without the original, we cannot honor your paper."

Harli snatched the copy out of the man's hand. "This is incompetence. We should be able to trust the courthouse to keep important papers. A man's life is at risk and all you can say is that you can't find the contract."

Manuel leaned his head over. "It is just a paper, senora," he said. "How can a man's life be in danger?"

Harli shot him a nasty look. "The true owner of this land has been kidnapped. The person who bought the entire property wants him and the rest of the villagers to move out. They have a legal right to be there, however, and we are trying to prove this point."

Manuel slunk back to his chair with a sheepish look. "Kidnapped?" he asked. "I did not know." He went back to filing papers.

Harli scoffed. "Yes, *kidnapped.* And if we don't find him, they might kill him. Nobody seems to want to help us!" She grabbed JC by the arm and said, "Let's go!"

Back in the van, Harli asked JC to guide her to one of the shops that bought crops from his father. JC pointed to a little store on the corner of the same street. "This is one," he said.

They drove down the street and stopped in front of the door. They walked inside and went to the counter. JC asked the girl at the counter to get the owner. She nodded and walked to the back. Soon a man walked out and smiled when he recognized JC.

"JC, my boy, how can I help you?" he asked.

"Hola, Rafael," JC said. "Please meet Harli. We want to ask some questions."

"Of course," Rafael answered as he reached out to shake Harli's hand. "Hola, Harli."

"Hola, Rafael," Harli answered. "Thank you for your time. You know Juan Carlos, right?"

"*Si,* yes!" Rafael replied. "He is a good, reliable man. Always brings me quality produce."

"Did you see him last Friday?" Harli asked.

"*Si,*" said Rafael. "He come and bring his delivery just like always. Right on time."

Harli wrote this down in her notebook. "Do you know where he went next?" she asked.

"He always go to the store about five blocks over after he visit me," Rafael said.

"Is there anything else you can tell me about that visit?" asked Harli. "Did he seem upset or worried?"

"No," Rafael replied. "He was happy like always. No problems."

Harli continued writing in her notebook. "Gracias, Rafael," she said. She handed him her business card. "If you think of anything else, please call me."

Rafael took the card and nodded. "*Si,* of course," he said. "Is something wrong?"

"He's been taken," JC said angrily. "We don't know where he is or if he is safe. Harli is trying to help us."

Rafael's face fell. "*Lo siento,* I'm sorry," he said. "I will help however I can."

The next stop was equally disappointing. The store owner repeated almost the exact same words as the previous store owner.

As they walked into the last store, the owner, Gabriella, greeted them with a friendly smile. She extended her hand to JC, but he did not reciprocate. He asked angrily, "Was my Papa here last Friday?"

Gabriella looked confused. *"Si,* he was here," she answered. "Why are you so upset?"

Harli interjected. "I'm Harli Chase," she said. "I am helping JC's family. Juan Carlos has been taken, and we do not know where he is. We are trying to find him. JC is just worried."

Gabriella nodded understandingly. "Ah, I see," she said. "Juan Carlos came on Friday. He very happy about new baby. He talk on and on about if it will be boy or girl."

"So, nothing seemed wrong?" Harli asked.

"No, nothing," Gabriella answered.

Harli sighed. "Okay, thank you," she said. She added with exasperation, "If you think of anything else, please call me." She gave Gabriella her business card.

JC and Harli started walking toward the door when Gabriella called them back. "We see his truck," she said. "We think so anyway." "Where?" JC asked eagerly.

"Sugar factory," Gabriella answered. "We not know why his truck is there."

"The green one, with wood sides?" JC questioned.

"Si, I think so," Gabriella said. "Hard to tell. It sit next to back entrance that is so dark. We drive by every day on our way to work and home. It was still there today," Gabriella added.

Harli excitedly shook Gabriella's hand. "Gracias!" she practically yelled. "JC, do you know where the sugar factory is?"

"Si," he answered. "Let's go!"

They ran out of the store still thanking the owner. They jumped into the van and Harli allowed JC to drive to the sugar factory. When they arrived, they circled around to the back to see if the truck was still there.

Harli strained her eyes to look and saw a vehicle sitting by the door. "Is that it?" she asked JC.

"I need to get close," JC said. "It looks like it, but I will know when I see the bumper."

They drove up to the parked truck and JC hopped out of the van to look at the back bumper. "It's our truck!" he yelled enthusiastically.

Harli hurriedly climbed out of the van. "How do you know?" she asked.

"When Carlita learn to drive she crash into the tractor," JC explained. "The bumper has red paint from the tractor and a big dent." He pointed to a large indentation in the bumper that had flecks of red paint. "See?"

Harli opened the driver's side door. "JC, come tell me if anything looks out of place or missing," she said. "But try not to touch anything. We will want the police to dust for fingerprints."

JC inspected the interior of the truck. He saw his father's coffee mug sitting in the drink holder and his sunglasses in the seat. There was a sticker on the dash that Natalia had given him. Nothing seemed to be missing, other than his father. He looked at Harli with disappointment.

Harli looked over the interior also and tried to see if there was any evidence that could have been left behind. She noticed a pair of fingernail clippers on the floor of the passenger's side. She took out her phone and took a photo before she pointed to them and asked JC, "Do these belong to your father?"

"I don't know," JC answered. "Maybe?"

Harli finished taking pictures of the interior. Then, JC and Harli looked at the bed of the truck. Harli pointed to a red speck on the inside of one of the wood rails. "That might be blood," she said quietly to herself.

JC overheard her. "Blood?!" he asked frantically. "Did they hurt my papa?"

Harli turned around. "Don't panic," she said. "It might not even be blood. But we need to consider all possibilities." She worked her way around the truck taking pictures of everything helpful, including the red paint from the tractor. She prayed the police would be able to find something to help them find Juan Carlos.

"We need to tell the police that the truck is here," Harli told JC.

"But they won't help!" JC protested.

"Finding your father's truck could spur them to action," Harli stated. "This could be quality evidence if they process it correctly. We can't take anything because that would be considered tampering. We have to follow the law. And if they still don't acknowledge that he is missing, we at least know where the truck is located."

JC hung his shoulders. "We can't even take the truck back to the village?"

"I'm afraid not," Harli said. "I'm sorry, but we cannot risk doing anything that might jeopardize finding your father. We do things by the book or not at all. Once the police process the evidence, we will be able to take the truck home."

JC drove them to the police station and once there, Harli asked to speak with a detective about a missing person report.

They spoke with the first available detective, giving him details about finding the truck and Juan Carlos's movements the morning he disappeared. While this was happening, a detective at another desk overheard their conversation. He quietly slipped off to a different room to make a phone call. "You have to move the truck," he said when his accomplice answered. "It's been found by the family.

Chapter Fifteen

Juan Carlos awoke to the sound of Andre dropping a tray of food into the cell. "Good morning, amigo. Gracias, *Dios lo bendiga.*"

"God bless me?" Andre asked. "Keep your 'God bless you' stuff to yourself. God has not blessed me. And quit calling me your friend!"

Juan Carlos smiled. "God has indeed blessed you, *mi* amigo," he said. "You have a wife and children, yes? Tell me about your family."

Andre looked annoyed. "Why do you care about my family?"

"I am just trying to get to know you," said Juan Carlos. "I do not have much else to do here. And what else do you have to entertain yourself?"

Andre rolled his eyes. "I guess you have a point," he grunted. "My wife's name is Delfini and my children are Paulo and Elena. There! Are you happy now?"

"How old are Paulo and Elena?" Juan Carlos asked.

"You don't give up, do you?" Andre snapped. Juan Carlos simply grinned.

"Fine," Andre consented. "Paulo is seven and Elena is four."

"My Natalia is four," Juan Carlos answered. "She is a jewel."

Andre jumped back from the cell door. "I see what you are doing!" he yelled. "You are trying to make me feel sorry for you! Well, it won't work so just stop trying. As a matter of fact, quit talking to me."

"If you wish," Juan Carlos said. "As I said, I was just passing the time. If you choose to talk again, you know where to find me, amigo." He opened his Bible and began reading to himself.

Andre sat quietly for approximately forty-five minutes and then he turned back toward the cage. "Why are you being so kind to me?" he asked. "I am holding you captive. You are supposed to hate me."

Juan Carlos looked up from his Bible. "I choose not to hate you, amigo," he said. "God tells us to love and not hate." Juan Carlos flipped through his Bible. "Here it is. Matthew five, forty-three and forty-four. 'You have heard that it was said, "Love your neighbor and hate your enemy." But I tell you, love your enemies and pray for those who persecute you.'"

Andre scoffed. "How can you choose not to hate? Don't you just feel that without choosing?"

"No, my friend," Juan Carlos responded. "When I experienced the love of God through His Son, Jesus, I understood that God chooses to love me. Because of this, He asks me to choose to love others. It goes beyond feeling. I am showing God's love to people when I choose to love also."

"Ridiculous! I can tell you; I hate my boss and feel no love for him at all!" Andre stated firmly.

"I understand," said Juan Carlos. "But that hatred is based upon your boss's actions, I'm supposing. God's love for us is not reliant upon our actions, but His choice to love no matter what. When you are determined to show love despite someone else's actions, it changes you. What has your boss done to anger you so?"

"He's a bad man. He talks down to me because my skin is not white. He's trying to steal land, and he kidnaps people," Andre replied. "I don't think I can ever love him."

"Why do you work for him if you do not like his actions?" asked Juan Carlos. "Certainly, there are other jobs?"

"None that pays this well," Andre said. "I have to provide for my family."

"I can see why the money appeals to you," Juan Carlos said. "But it is a dangerous trade."

"Trade?" Andre asked.

"To gain the world just to lose your soul," answered Juan Carlos.

"I have my soul!" snapped Andre.

Juan Carlos paused and then spoke quietly. "God asks us to follow Him and in return, He saves our soul. Our soul will remain in heaven with Him for the remainder of time, after we die. However, the things of this earth will be gone. We will not have, or need, money or cars, or jewelry. To work for money means to serve the things of this world. To work for God means to serve Him and save your soul."

Andre laughed. "But we need money to survive. That doesn't make sense."

"Yes, we do," Juan Carlos acknowledged. "However, we rely on God to provide what we need. He will guide you to the right job just for you and it will address your needs perfectly."

"Whatever. Your God sounds bossy," replied Andre.

Juan Carlos laughed. "You could see it that way, if you choose. He does not force anyone to come to Him. He simply offers true life for anyone who wants to accept it. Do you force your children to love you?"

Andre stopped and thought about this for a moment. "Well, no, I don't suppose I do," he answered.

"That's the way God is with us. We are His children," Juan Carlos said. He held the Bible in the air toward Andre. "He gives us this book as an instruction manual for life because He loves us. He doesn't force us, He helps us."

There was silence between the two for several moments. Juan Carlos was pleased that he had given Andre something to think about. He began to softly sing praise to God.

Andre paced outside of the cell door. Suddenly he stopped and looked at Juan Carlos. "What do you mean we are His children?" he asked.

Juan Carlos stopped singing and smiled at Andre. "God has created each and every one of us. This makes us His children. However, we have sinned and separated ourselves from Him. When we accept the sacrifice of Jesus on the cross, we are reunited with God as His children. He cares for His children very much and makes sure that we have everything that we need."

"Hmph," Andre responded and continued pacing.

Juan Carlos said a silent prayer for Andre. *Father God, help Andre see how much You love him and help him to make his way to You. Use me while I am here to be Your vessel. In Jesus' mighty name, amen.*

Back at the police station Detective Sebastian Sanchez looked at Harli and JC and listened to their story. "Why haven't you reported this sooner?" he asked.

JC jumped out of the chair and yelled, "We did! We've come to you twice!" Harli put her hand on JC's arm and gently pulled him back down into his chair.

"Detective, what JC is trying to tell you is that there have been previous attempts made to inform the police and obtain their assistance," Harli informed him.

Detective Sanchez typed into his computer. "There is nothing here," he said. "This is strange. We have no information on a missing person named Juan Carlos Martinez."

"Nothing?" JC asked in disbelief.

The detective leaned over his desk and whispered. "We do have some here who are not always honest." He leaned back to the computer. "I will enter the report right now. I will need all of the details again, unfortunately. I apologize for that."

Harli placed her hand on JC's arm again. "We understand," she said before he could speak. She looked at him and said quietly, "JC, the other officers did not help you, but we have to trust this one. He seems honest."

Once the report had been submitted, Officer Sanchez handed them a business card and stood up. "Oh wait," he said as he reached back for the card. "Let me add my cell phone number on the back. Call me there if you need to reach me. Would you guys mind riding with me to show me where you saw the truck?"

The ride to the sugar factory was a quiet one. As they pulled up to the place where the truck had been they were greeted with a shocking sight.

"It was right there!" JC yelled as his face grew red.

"He's right," Harli affirmed. "The truck was placed right there. I took pictures. Where could it be now?"

Detective Sanchez shook his head. "If I have to guess, someone at the station heard that you found it and tipped off whoever took it. I will put out a "Be On The Lookout" alert for it. You said you have pictures. Did you get pictures of the license plate?"

Harli nodded and opened the picture app on her phone. She handed the phone to Sanchez. He flipped through the pictures. "These are great," he said. "Please send them to me?"

Harli agreed. "We also talked with the shop owners whom he sold produce to," she said. "They said everything was fine when he was there on Friday. He made all his scheduled stops and was not in any distress."

"That means he was taken on his way home," Sanchez said thoughtfully. "And his truck ended up here."

"What are we to do now?" JC asked angrily. "We are back to the start. We have nothing to go on!"

"We can investigate the factory," Detective Sanchez said. "I know the owner and I have police officers that I trust. Once I put the BOLO out on your dad's truck, I'll listen for any sightings.

"Thank you for your help," Harli said as she reached out to shake the hand of Officer Sanchez. She handed him her business card. "Please call me if you have any leads. I am going to be investigating on my own as well. It would be nice to work together."

"I would like that," Offer Sanchez said as he returned her handshake.

CHAPTER SIXTEEN

The villagers continued with their daily activities. The absence of Juan Carlos was felt, but they stayed busy to avoid sadness and worry. Jexi and Shaya helped with the kids at school. Jessie and Sharon helped Angelica clean her house and move furniture to make room for the new baby. Hunter and Ben helped the other men do the finishing work around the well to keep it stable and keep the ground around it from eroding. Jexi was astonished at how everyone worked together in such a seamless fashion.

Harli and JC returned in the late afternoon. The team gathered to hear what they had discovered but could tell by the looks on their faces that the day had not gone as well as they had hoped. Harli shared with them the news of locating the truck and talking with Detective Sanchez.

"One of the store owners told us she had seen the truck at the sugar factory, so we went to see for ourselves," Harli informed them. "JC verified that it was Juan Carlos's truck because it had a red paint smudge. We took pictures of everything we saw and then went to the police station."

"They did not have any information that we had reported Dad missing!" JC added, angrily. "The other police officers we talked to did nothing! But we met Detective Sanchez, and he helped us."

Harli continued, "When we got back to the sugar factory, the truck was gone! Gabriella said it had been there all week, and suddenly it was gone! So, here we are, back to having no leads."

Ken shook his head. "There are several corrupt police officers, unfortunately."

"My instincts tell me that we can trust Sanchez though," Harli mentioned. "He put out a BOLO on the truck and entered the information into the police system."

After a day filled with chores, the people built a bonfire and sat around it fellowshipping. Children roasted marshmallows, which was a special treat from Ken and Sharon, while adults talked with each other. It was a nice time for everyone to relax.

Harli's phone chirped and she looked to see who had texted her. It was Detective Sanchez. The text read, *"We need to talk. Can you meet me now?"*

"Now?" Harli replied. "It's late."

"Now. It's important," Sanchez wrote. "I'll come to the village."

"Okay," Harli wrote back. "Don't drive your police car. I'll explain when you get here."

The text Harli received read, "Okay. Be there in one hour."

Harli texted, "I'll let everyone else know you're coming so they don't worry when you arrive."

Harli notified the team that Detective Sanchez would be arriving soon and Sharon looked at her alarmed. "Why would he come all the way out here this late in the evening?"

"I don't know," Harli admitted. "But I'm sure it will be okay. He will not be in a police car, so hopefully the villagers will not be scared."

While they waited for the detective to arrive, Hunter busied himself with some of the children. Jexi noticed that he was holding a guitar that appeared to be homemade and was teaching some of the kids to play simple chords. She walked to them and listened to their interactions for a minute. When they paused, she asked him, "Where did you get the guitar?"

"I made it," Hunter answered. "I used some of the cardboard from boxes and rubber bands to make the strings. It's not exact, but the idea is the same. The kids seem to really enjoy learning how to play."

Jexi smiled as her heart fluttered. She hadn't realized that Hunter was so creative or that he was so good with children. "That's sweet of you," she told him.

"Dante is learning quickly," Hunter said. "And Diego is pretty good too. If they ever get their hands on real guitars, they will be able to play with ease."

Jexi sat next to him. "Can I join you?" she asked.

"Of course!" Hunter answered. "Would you like to learn?"

Jexi shook her head. "Nah, let the kids play. There is plenty of time for me to learn. I'll just watch."

Hunter continued showing the kids how to place their fingers on the strings and frets of the guitar. As Jexi observed, she found herself thinking that Hunter would make a really good father someday.

The sound of tires on gravel jolted her out of her thoughts. She joined the others as they approached the car. Detective Sanchez parked and exited the car. "Good evening," he said. "Sorry to interrupt so late, but this is important. Is there somewhere we can talk?"

Ken nodded. "We can talk in the schoolhouse. It's this way."

JC saw the group head toward the schoolhouse and jogged to catch up. "Detective?" he asked. "What are you doing here? Did you find my papa?"

The detective shook his head. "No, not yet. Let's get inside and I'll fill you in."

The group filed in and found seats in proximity to Detective Sanchez. When everyone was seated, he started. "Something strange happened when I got back to the station this afternoon. I opened my computer files to add the information about the missing truck. The file is GONE. All of it. There is no record of the report. Again."

Harli pounded her hand on the bench in anger. "Gone? How?"

"Another detective came up to me while I was looking and he said that I must not have saved it correctly into the system," Sanchez explained. "I know I saved it. From now on though, we must keep everything on paper to keep it safe."

JC looked puzzled. "Did someone erase it?" he asked.

Detective Sanchez looked at him. "Yes," he said. "I can't explain it any other way. As I said, not all the officers are honest." He turned his attention to Harli. "Why did you ask that I drive my own car?" he asked her.

"A couple of reasons," Harli answered. "One, I didn't want the others to get scared. For good reason, they don't always trust the police and it could have caused a panic. Two, the village is being watched."

"What do you mean by 'watched'? How do you know this?" Sanchez asked.

"The new owner, McGreggor, has his henchmen driving around the village with guns periodically," Ken said. "They seem to be watching everything we do."

"Do you know they are McGreggor's men?" Sanchez asked.

Jessie scoffed. "No, but who else could they be?" she asked. "No one else is concerned with this village."

Sanchez nodded. "I see."

"So, you see how serious this is," Harli said.

"*Si*, I do," said Sanchez. "I will do the best I can to help you. For now, I will investigate the few pieces of information we do have. If you hear anything, call me. I will be in touch."

"What do we do?" JC asked.

"Unfortunately, there is nothing you can do right now," Sanchez said. "I trust my captain, so I will talk to him about putting out the BOLO for the truck again. I will also get a search warrant for the sugar factory. I promise that I will inform you of anything I find. I am going to go home now."

"Wait," Harli said. "I know there is something fishy going on with the county clerk's office too. Remember the land deed has gone missing as well. Maybe you can talk to Manuel. He acted like he knew more than he was saying."

"Yes," said Sanchez. "I will have to wait until Monday to question him because they are not open on the weekend."

"Can't you find his address and go to his house?" Shaya asked.

"No disrespect, senorita," Sanchez said. "But Manuel is a very common name here. Without his last name, it would be hard to find him."

Harli snapped her fingers several times. "Oh, I know his last name . . . it was on his nameplate at the courthouse. Oh, what was that name?" She squeezed her eyes tight and thought for a moment. "I remember! Escobar!"

Detective Sanchez wrote Manuel's name in his notebook. "That gives me a good place to start. Thank you. Get some sleep tonight." He looked at Harli. "I will contact you tomorrow."

"I'll walk you to your car," Harli offered.

Sanchez smiled.

CHAPTER SEVENTEEN

The next day, Sanchez talked with his captain and informed him of what was happening with Juan Carlos and the missing reports. The captain assured Sanchez that he would look into the other officers in the department. He quickly granted the search warrant for the sugar factory. While the captain was gathering a team to carry out the warrant, Sanchez located Manuel Escobar and went to his house to talk with him.

He found Manuel outside pulling weeds in his flower bed. He walked up to him and introduced himself. "I am Detective Sanchez with the Honduras Police Department. I am investigating the disappearance of a village man, and I would like to ask you a few questions."

Manuel's face turned white. "I know nothing, senor," he said.

"I have not even told you who I am looking for," Sanchez replied. "How can you be sure you know nothing?"

Manuel froze. "Um, I do not know, senor. I am just a clerk. I only know paper. I don't know about missing people."

"This man's name is Juan Carlos Martinez. He has been gone for over a week. There is a document that should be at the courthouse that gives his family and friends the legal right to stay on their land, but it seems to be missing. Several people have come to the courthouse asking to see this document. Do you know anything about this?"

"Of course not, senor," answered Manuel. "I do not know what has happened to the document."

"Are you sure?" questioned Sanchez.

"*Si,* senor," Manuel said as he looked at the ground.

Detective Sanchez did not believe him, but he could see that Manuel was not going to give him any information. He handed him a business card. "If you know anything or hear of anything, please call me. This man's life could be in grave danger."

Manuel did not look up as he shook the detective's hand. *"Si,* of course," he mumbled.

Sanchez turned and walked toward his car.

Manuel stood in the garden staring at the flowers. A voice in the back of his head told him, *You should have been honest! You lied to a detective!* He shook his head and argued with himself. *I do not know how dangerous these men are! They could cause me more harm than the police. I cannot tell what I know. I must stay quiet! But I do not want this man to be hurt.*

Detective Sanchez glanced at Manuel one last time to see if he had a change of heart, but Manuel continued to stare at the flowers as Sanchez got into the patrol car.

Sanchez decided to check on the status of the search warrant. He called his captain before he left Manuel's house.

"The warrant is secured," the captain said as he answered the phone.

"Gracias," said Sanchez. "I am going to the factory now. Can someone meet me there with the warrant?"

"Si! I will send the teams and the warrant," replied the captain.

Sanchez ended the call and immediately dialed Harli's number. When she answered, he said, "We have the warrant. I am going to the sugar factory now and I will update you later."

"I can come right away," Harli said. "No," Sanchez said. "It might not be safe. We have trained men to handle this. Stay there, I will call you."

At the sugar factory, the police had gathered and were waiting for Sanchez's lead. "We are ready on your signal," said the leader of the Comando de Operaciones Especiales, Honduras's SWAT team.

Sanchez sent two teams to the back of the factory and two teams to storm the front. On his command, the teams entered the factory and set about clearing each room and level.

After a few minutes, Sanchez heard from the head of each team that the building was cleared and secure. After the last walkie call had come through, one officer ran up to him and yelled, "Detective, we found the truck!"

Sanchez dialed Harli's number again, as he followed the officer. When she answered, he quickly stated, "We found the truck at the sugar factory," and disconnected the call without hearing her response.

Sanchez ordered the team to process every inch of Juan Carlos's truck carefully. "Take pictures, dust for fingerprints, and comb for DNA," he ordered. "I want this done right. We have to find this man."

From behind him, Sanchez heard a female voice. "Make sure you get those fingernail clippers. Those do not belong to Juan Carlos."

Detective Sanchez whirled around to see Harli standing there. "I told you not to come," he snapped.

"Well, I ignored you," Harli snapped back. "This is important to me."

"It is important to me, too," Sanchez said. "I have to do this by the book, or it is a waste of time. Plus, you didn't know how dangerous this could have been. You should have waited."

"Lighten up, cowboy," Harli quipped. "I am a trained professional and know how to handle myself and a crime scene. I promise not to be in your way. But I am not leaving."

Sanchez softened his tone. "I know. And I appreciate that. But if you interfere with a police investigation, it could jeopardize this work. Plus, I did not want you to get hurt." Sanchez blushed and continued. "But since you're here, you can stand over there where we are collecting the evidence. Let me know if there is anything that wasn't there when you first found the truck."

Harli walked to the bags of evidence but did not notice anything new. She wandered back to the truck and began to look it over. When she got to the driver's side door, she slid on a glove and gently opened it. On the inside of the door near the handle was a greasy palm smear. "Detective!" she called.

Sanchez ran over. "What? Find something?"

"Yeah," Harli answered. "This palm smear wasn't here last time. It must be from whoever moved the truck."

Sanchez waved over the DNA and fingerprint technicians. "Get this palm smear," he ordered. "Prints and DNA. I want it all." He pulled down the visor and a set of keys fell into the seat. "These keys too," he said.

"How long will it take to process all of this in the lab?" Harli asked.

Sanchez looked concerned. "I do not know. I am afraid to use the police lab because the evidence could disappear, just like the report. I don't know who to trust."

Harli scowled. "We will have to hire an independent lab."

Sanchez nodded. "Yes, that would be a good idea. In the meantime, we have made great progress. Finding this truck was a win for us today. By the way, I spoke with Manuel. I agree that he is suspicious."

"Got nothing, huh?" Harli asked.

"He clammed up," Sanchez answered. "I'll keep at him though. Once we are finished here, I will have one of the officers take the truck back to the village. We will not need it anymore. I recommend hiding it if you can."

Harli smiled. "This will make JC and the rest of the family very happy," she said. She pulled Detective Sanchez in for a hug before she realized what she was doing. She released him quickly. "Oh, sorry."

"Don't be," Detective Sanchez replied.

Juan Carlos ate his dinner in silence as Andre sat outside of his cell. Once he was done, he asked Andre quietly, "What day is it?"

Andre replied. "Saturday."

"Do you think you would be able to take me to church tomorrow morning?" Juan Carlos asked. "I miss being at church very much."

Andre sneered at him. "You can't be serious?" he asked incredulously.

"*Si,* I am serious," answered Juan Carlos.

"No, you aren't going to church," Andre said. "You are a prisoner, remember?"

"Oh," Juan Carlos said sadly.

There was silence for several minutes. Then Andre spoke. "I will bring you a radio. If you can find a preacher to listen to."

Juan Carlos smiled. *"¡Gracias,* senor!"

"Don't get so sappy on me, old man," said Andre. "Are you done with your food?"

"Si," Juan Carlos said as he passed the plate back to him. "My Sophia's birthday is coming. She will be ten years old."

"Don't push your luck," Andre said. He took the plate and turned toward the door. "See you tomorrow," he added, as he walked out of the area and his replacement entered.

CHAPTER EIGHTEEN

"Here is your radio," Andre said coldly as he entered the temporary prison of Juan Carlos the next morning.

Juan Carlos was overwhelmed. "Oh, *gracias,* senor! Gracias!"

"I told you, don't get so sappy," Andre said. "Good luck getting any signal and finding a sermon," he said with a laugh.

Juan Carlos turned the knobs of the radio until a station could be heard loud and clear. He listened for a moment to hear what was being broadcast. He heard a strong voice, praying.

"Dios es bueno!" he cheered. "Praise the Lord!"

"You found something?" Andre asked skeptically.

"Si, si," Juan Carlos said. "Now, shh."

Both men listened as the man talking on the radio finished his prayer and began to preach in Spanish. "Once there was a young man named Saul. He hated God's people and set out to kill them and wipe them off the earth. He persecuted them day and night. Open your Bible to Acts nine, one and two: 'Meanwhile, Saul was still breathing out murderous threats against the Lord's disciples. He went to the high priest and asked him for letters to the synagogues in Damascus, so that if he found any there who belonged to the Way, whether men or women, he might take them as prisoners to Jerusalem.' He was a dangerous man. Many people feared him. Does anyone know then, what happened to this young man; what became of him? Look at Acts nine, verses three through six, and verses eight and nine. 'As he neared Damascus on his journey, suddenly a light from heaven flashed around him. He fell to the ground and heard a voice say to him, "Saul, Saul, why do you persecute me?" "Who are you, Lord?" Saul asked. "I am Jesus, whom you are persecuting," he replied. "Now

get up and go into the city, and you will be told what you must do."
Saul got up from the ground, but when he opened his eyes, he could
see nothing. So, they led him by the hand into Damascus. For three
days he was blind, and did not eat or drink anything.' God led him to
the home of a believer who fed him and took care of him. Meanwhile,
God spoke to a man named Ananias and told him to go and witness
to him. Ananias was terrified because he knew of Saul and his hatred
for Christians. Ananias trusted God to protect him so he went to Saul
and laid his hands upon him. His sight was returned as something like
scales fell off. Now listen to what God did with this man! Still in Acts
nine, verses twenty through twenty-two. 'At once he began to preach
in the synagogues that Jesus is the Son of God. All those who heard
him were astonished and asked, "Isn't he the man who raised havoc
in Jerusalem among those who call on this name? And hasn't he come
here to take them as prisoners to the chief priests?" Yet Saul grew
more and more powerful and baffled the Jews living in Damascus by
proving that Jesus is the Messiah.' If God can do that with a murderer,
what can He do with you? Certainly, your actions are no worse than
those of that man! Saul began to go by his Greek name of Paul and
became one of the most dedicated of the apostles. He also went on to
write several books of the Bible. God can use anyone who is willing
to serve Him. God loves you and no matter what you have done, He
can use you for His kingdom!"

Sitting on a church pew in town with his Abuela, Manuel listened
to the same message that was being broadcast to Juan Carlos's cell.
He was astonished at how God could easily forgive a man who mur-
dered those who followed Jesus. He thought of his own circumstances. He sat on this church pew pretending to be a good person. He had
done something terrible. Could God forgive him? Sure He could, but
would He?

The pastor preaching continued. "Repent! To repent means to turn
away from your sin and follow the Lord. If you believe in your heart
that God is Lord of all, that Jesus rose from the dead, ask forgiveness

for your sins, and then accept Him as your personal Lord and Savior, you will be welcomed into His family with open arms. You will be forgiven, and you can then live for Him! If you do not know how to do this, I will lead you in a sinner's prayer. Follow my lead."

Manuel decided right then to say this prayer and commit his life to the Lord. He had done terrible things, and he must make things right.

The pastor continued. "Father God, I have sinned. I believe that You are Lord of all, and I repent of my sins. I am so sorry. I believe that You rose from the grave, and I accept You as my Lord and Savior. Please forgive me and guide me. Amen."

Andre had been listening to the sermon along with Juan Carlos. He was intrigued by God's forgiveness. *Is this real?* he thought. *Could God forgive me?* He turned his back to Juan Carlos and whispered the words along with the pastor. When he finished, he felt different. He couldn't describe the change, but he knew that he was not the same man he had been.

When the pastor completed a closing prayer, Juan Carlos switched the radio off and lifted it toward Andre. Andre's back was to him. "Andre?" he called gently.

Andre turned around. Juan Carlos saw in his eyes that he had changed. He held the radio out to return it, but Andre held up his hand. "Keep it," Andre said. "It might help ease some of the loneliness. Just don't play it when others are around. This will be our secret."

"Oh, gracias, gracias, senor!" Juan Carlos exclaimed. "Did you enjoy the pastor's sermon?"

"Actually, *si,*" said Andre. "I don't understand everything, but I can see why this God is so appealing to you."

"He is my everything," Juan Carlos said. "He can be yours, too."

"Easy, old man," Andre said. "Listen to your radio. I'll be right back."

Moments later, Andre returned with a piece of paper and a pencil. "I can't make any promises, *comprendes,*" he began, "but write a letter to your Sophia for her birthday and I will try to get it to her."

"Really?" asked Juan Carlos.

"*Si,* just hurry up," said Andre. "I don't want to get caught."

Juan Carlos hurriedly scribbled a note onto the paper for his beloved daughter and handed it back to Andre. "Her birthday is on Wednesday," he said. "Gracias, amigo."

Andre shoved the note into his pocket. *"De nada,"* he muttered.

At his house, Manuel looked for the business card that Sanchez had given him. He finally found it lying face down on top of his dresser. He picked it up and stared at it for a while. *Should I really do this?* he asked himself. The answer came swiftly. *Yes. This is the right thing to do. This is what God would want you to do.* He took his cell phone out of his pocket, nervously dialed the detective's number, and waited shakily while it rang.

"Hola, Detective Sanchez," he heard.

"Detective, this is Manuel Escobar," he said quietly. "I need to meet with you. Someplace private. Not the police station or my house."

"Do you know the coffeehouse on the corner near the police station?" Sanchez asked. "We can meet there. One hour."

"Okay," said Manuel and he ended the call. His hands were trembling, but he knew he was doing what had to be done. He prepared to go out and meet the detective.

Detective Sanchez punched Harli's number as soon as he ended the call with Manuel. When she answered, he quickly said, "We may have a lead. Meet me at the coffeehouse on the corner, near the police station in an hour."

"Hello to you too," Harli sarcastically responded.

"Sorry," Sanchez apologized. "I got excited about the lead."

"Do you want me to come alone?" Harli asked.

"That would be best," the detective answered. "I don't know exactly where this will take us yet."

"Got it," Harli said. "See you in an hour." She ended the call and went to find Ken and Sharon. She would need their vehicle once again.

Harli walked into the coffeehouse and spotted Detective Sanchez sitting across from a man. She approached cautiously and realized it was Manuel Escobar. "Good afternoon, Detective Sanchez." She paused and landed her gaze on Manuel. "And Mr. Escobar." She sat down next to Sanchez, who had scooted over to make room.

"Manuel has something to tell us," Sanchez said. "Go ahead."

Manuel cleared his throat. "I, um, I need to be honest about something," he began tentatively. He scanned the room before he spoke next. "I don't want to go to jail, and I don't want any harm to come to me or my family." He paused and took a deep breath.

"I can't promise either one, but I will try my best to keep you safe," Sanchez said. "Go on."

"I was paid to destroy the contract for the villagers' land in Aldea Gracia," he said in a rush.

"I knew it!" yelled Harli as she pounded the table with her fist. Several patrons looked at them and Manuel slunk down into his seat.

Sanchez shushed her. "Let's hear him out first, okay?" Harli nodded and regained her composure. "Who paid you, Manuel?" asked Sanchez.

"I do not know, senor," answered Manuel. "He would not tell me his name. He said that I was to destroy the document, or they would hurt my family. I was so scared of losing my *abuela* and my mama. So, I took the papers."

"And you destroyed them," finished Sanchez.

"No, senor," said Manuel. "I could not do such a thing. I hid them and only told these people that they were destroyed."

Harli cheered aloud and once again drew the attention of other people in the coffeehouse.

"You have to control yourself!" Sanchez whispered.

"Sorry," said Harli. "I was just so excited when I heard that."

"Where is the document?" Sanchez asked.

"In the basement of the courthouse," answered Manuel. "In a box of storage."

"We have to get those papers, Sanchez," said Harli.

"I know," Sanchez responded. "But we must be careful about how we go about it. These people have eyes everywhere and will know what we are doing if we just barge in there. We need a plan. They will know who we are right away."

"They haven't seen Jexi, Shaya, or Ben," Harli offered.

"Smart," said Sanchez. "We will get two of them to go in. They must be discreet about it; they can't yell out names or anything. Can they handle something like this?"

"Let's find out," Harli suggested. "Come back to the village with me."

Sanchez looked at Manuel. "You will be at work on Monday?" he asked.

"Si, senor," said Manuel.

"Good," said Sanchez. "Can you get there early to get the papers from the basement? Put them in an envelope labeled *'Birth Records'* ahead of time and have them in your desk drawer. We will get two people to ask for those papers tomorrow. You will not recognize them, but they will be American. They will ask for an application for a birth certificate. You will pretend to get that application for them but give them the contract papers instead. Can you do that?"

Manuel nodded. "I think so," he said. "Nobody else in the office knows I took the papers."

Harli took Manuel's hand. "You are helping us, and we greatly appreciate your efforts. Thank you for making the right choice."

Sanchez smiled. "We have a plan then. Harli, I will follow you to the village to talk with the others. Manuel, it will be over soon. Wait here for ten minutes after we leave. I will talk with my captain about keeping you and your family safe." Sanchez reached out to shake Manuel's hand. "Gracias, amigo."

Manuel remained in the booth after they left, just as Sanchez had ordered. He continued drinking his coffee and soon felt a sense of calm wash over him.

CHAPTER NINETEEN

Once Harli and Detective Sanchez explained the plan to Shaya and Jexi, the girls agreed to it immediately. Harli reminded them that it could be dangerous and to make sure to be calm yet discreet. They did a few practice runs to help prepare the girls for their roles.

Jexi lay in bed that night, tossing and turning. She had become nervous and was unable to fall asleep. She didn't want to disturb Jessie, Shaya, or Harli, so she quietly slipped on her shoes and stepped outside. As she stood, breathing the fresh air to help her calm down, she saw a man sitting at the picnic table near the fire pit. He had his head bowed and she thought he might be sleeping. She took a few steps towards him and his head popped up. His eyes reached hers and she immediately recognized them as Hunter's.

"Oh, hi," she said nervously. "I didn't mean to disturb you. I'll head back."

"No, you don't have to do that," Hunter answered. "Please, join me."

Jexi sat down opposite him at the picnic table. "Is everything okay?" she asked.

"Yes," he replied. "I was just praying for your mission tomorrow. I know it might be risky, so I was praying for God's protection over you and Shaya."

She reached out and touched his arm. "Hunter, that is so thoughtful. I am a little uneasy about it, so your prayers are appreciated."

Hunter looked into her eyes and her heart melted. "Is that why you are out here right now?" he asked.

"Yeah, I couldn't sleep," Jexi responded. "I didn't want to disturb the others, so I thought I'd get some fresh air."

"I wasn't finished with my prayer," Hunter started. "We can finish it together if you would like. It might help you sleep better."

Jexi was astounded at his kindness. She wondered, *Can a guy like this even be real?* She smiled at him. "That would be great, thank you," she said.

Hunter took her hands in his as he began to pray. "Father God, we know Your hand is on us, always. Please send a wave of peace over Jexi. Give her a restful night and keep them safe tomorrow. We know that You are perfect in all Your ways. Thank You for loving us. Amen."

Jexi opened her eyes, and Hunter was still holding her hands. She did not want to pull away. She felt so comfortable and at ease when she was with him. After a moment, Hunter gently pulled his hands away. "I guess you'd better get to sleep. You have a big morning ahead."

Jexi nodded. "Yeah, you're right. Thank you for praying, I appreciate it."

Hunter winked at her. "Anytime," he said. "It's what I do." He stood up and walked toward the hut he was staying in. "Good night!"

Jexi called after him. "Hunter!" She paused when he stopped to look back at her. "I'm glad you are here."

"Me too," Hunter answered and walked into his hut.

Jexi walked back into her hut and took off her shoes. Immediately, she felt extremely sleepy. She looked up to heaven. "Thank You," As soon as she pulled the covers up to her neck, she was out.

The next morning, Jexi and Shaya both awoke with a sense of purpose. Neither one could eat much for breakfast, but they were excited about doing their part to help the village of Aldea Gracia.

Harli approached them. "Okay girls, you remember the plan, right?" The girls nodded. "I am going to drive you to town. I will park at the coffee shop; Sanchez will meet me there. You two will walk to the courthouse. Look for the nameplate that says Manuel Escobar; approach his window and ask for birth certificate papers."

"We know, Harli," said Jexi. "We've gone over it a hundred times."

"This isn't a game," Harli responded harshly. "These people are dangerous. They've already kidnapped one man, who's to say they won't do it again? Or worse? You have to take this seriously and stay safe!"

Shaya waved her hands between the other two women. "Both of you need to chill. We know this is not a game, but we are also very prepared. When we get the papers, we will meet you and Sanchez back at the coffeehouse."

Harli breathed a calming breath. "Right. I know you are aware of the danger, but I worry, okay?"

Jexi spoke up. "I'm sorry, Harli. I didn't mean to act like this wasn't serious. I guess I'm a little nervous."

"Good," said Harli. "That will help keep you on your toes."

Ben, Hunter, and the rest of the gang came to see them off. Ben hugged Shaya closely and whispered in her ear. "I still wish you weren't doing this."

Shaya whispered back, "I know, but God will keep us safe, you know that. We will be back this evening. I love you."

"I love you, too," Ben whispered.

Hunter and Jexi looked at each other awkwardly for a moment. Hunter held up his hand for a high five. "Be safe," he said.

"We will," Jexi responded as she returned the high five. She giggled at his silly send-off but was grateful he didn't say anything mushy. She wasn't sure her nerves would hold if he said anything sweet.

The group made it to the coffee shop and Harli reviewed the plan one more time. The two girls took a deep breath and headed in the direction of the coffeehouse.

"You nervous?" Shaya asked Jexi, as they exited the van.

"Yeah, a little," Jexi said. "You?"

"Yeah, me too," Shaya answered.

The two walked in silence the rest of the way.

Once inside the courthouse, a guard asked them what their purpose was for being there. Jexi croaked out, "Birth certificate papers, please."

The guard gruffly pointed in the direction of two windows and turned back around.

Jexi and Shaya walked toward the windows and saw that only one of them was open. The second window had been temporarily closed for the clerk to take a break. They hoped that the open window was Manuel's. They cautiously looked at the nameplate and saw it plain as day: *"Manuel Escobar."* They both breathed a sigh of relief at the same time.

They stood in the line and were thankful that there were only two people ahead of them. When it was their turn, Shaya spoke first. "We would like papers for a birth certificate, please."

Manuel's eyes opened wide, and he froze for a brief moment. Finally, he regained his composure, looked around, and then asked in a grave whisper, "Did Sanchez send you?"

Shaya nodded. "Yes, that's correct," she said out loud. "We would like birth certificate papers, please."

"Oh, yes, birth certificate papers," Manuel said shakily. "Of course, I have them right here." He reached down into the bottom drawer and pulled out an envelope. He handed the envelope to Shaya and said, "Here you go."

Shaya took the envelope and said, "Thank you, sir. You don't know how important these birth certificate papers are to us." The girls turned around to walk out the door.

As they neared the front entrance, the guard spoke loudly enough to startle them. "Stop here for a moment, *por favor,"* he said. Both girls' hearts pounded in their chests. Jexi was sure the whole courthouse could hear hers thumping.

Shaya seemed to be the epitome of calm as they stopped in front of the guard. Jexi's thoughts were racing a mile a minute as she was sure they had gotten caught. *Oh no, this is it. We're going to die. This is the end. Oh God, please let my family know how much I love them.* She could feel herself begin to sweat.

The guard looked at them. "Did you find what you were needing?" he asked. He looked directly at Jexi. "You look sick. Are you okay?"

Jexi shook her head but couldn't speak. Shaya thought quickly. "She just had a baby," Shaya told the guard. "She still isn't feeling very well yet."

The guard shrugged in understanding. "Oh, I see," he said. "Well, I hope you found what you needed."

"We most certainly did," Shaya responded. "The service here is nice and quick. Thank you!"

"De nada," answered the guard. "Have a nice day." The girls rushed out to head to the coffeehouse.

Once they cleared the courthouse entrance, they stopped for a breath. Jexi put her hand on her heart. "I thought we were for sure going to die!"

"Seriously, you overreact way too much," Shaya said sarcastically. "You almost blew our cover."

"But I didn't," Jexi answered. "By the way, good thinking back there."

"Thanks," said Shaya. "Someone had to stay calm and rescue the situation."

They entered the coffeehouse and saw Sanchez sitting with Harli. They joined them at the table and began to giggle.

"What can possibly be so funny?" Harli asked.

"Nervous Nellie over here almost messed it all up when the guard stopped us," Shaya said. "But I saved the day."

Harli's questions flew out of her mouth. "What? The guard stopped you? Why? What happened?"

"He just wanted to know if we found what we needed," Shaya said. Then she pointed to Jexi. "But this one thought we had been caught for sure. The guard asked her why she looked so sick, and I told him that she'd just had a baby and wasn't feeling well."

"Clever! I'm impressed!" Harli commended.

Sanchez cleared his throat to stop the chatter. "Did you get the documents?" asked Sanchez.

"Sure did!" Shaya responded. She pulled them out of her bag and handed the papers to him.

He opened the envelope and surveyed the papers. He breathed a sigh of relief when he realized that these were indeed the actual contract papers. "We've got them," he said. "This is a small victory, but the battle isn't over. I'll keep these at *mi casa* since I don't know who I can trust at the station."

The four of them high-fived one another for a mission well executed.

CHAPTER TWENTY

That evening was full of celebration in the village. Everyone was overjoyed with having the proof of ownership they needed to stay on their land.

Sanchez attended the celebration at the request of Harli, but his mind was filled with what to do next. He did not join the festivities. Harli found him standing outside on the porch of the schoolhouse.

"Come inside! It's a celebration!" Harli invited.

"I am glad that we have the contract," Sanchez answered. "But we aren't finished yet. I am trying to figure out our next move. We are still waiting for the lab results from the truck. I am hopeful that we get a hit on the prints and DNA. Without that, we are still no closer to finding Juan Carlos."

While they were talking, a beat-up black truck drove into the village. The man drove up to the schoolhouse and parked. Sanchez and Harli both drew their guns. "Who are you?" Sanchez demanded.

"Por favor, senor," the man said as he turned off the truck. "I mean no harm. I have a letter from Juan Carlos."

"Get out of the truck, now!" Sanchez ordered. Harli covered him as he put the man in handcuffs. "What do you know about Juan Carlos? You need to start talking right now."

The man was in a panic. "Andre did not warn me about guns. I am just to deliver a letter."

"Who's Andre?" Harli asked.

"He is my cousin," the petrified man answered.

"Do you or he work for McGreggor?" Sanchez asked.

"McGreggor?" the man questioned. "I do not know anyone by that name."

"Don't play dumb with us!" Harli screamed. "You just happen to have a letter from a kidnapped man, and you don't know McGreggor? Yeah, right. How about the truth now?"

"Kid . . . kidnapped?" the man stammered.

"I asked once, and I won't ask again after this. What is your name?" said Sanchez.

"I am Alberto," the man quietly answered. *"Mi* amigos call me Bert. Andre is my cousin. I don't know anything about a kidnapping or even who Juan Carlos is, I promise. All Andre said was to come here and say I have a letter from him. I didn't know I would end up in handcuffs! *Lo siento* . . . I'm so sorry! I just want to go home."

Harli and Sanchez exchanged glances. By now, a few more people from the village had gathered outside to observe the commotion.

Sanchez addressed Alberto, "Where is the letter?"

Alberto answered, "In this pocket, on my shirt." He tilted his chin toward his chest.

Sanchez reached into the pocket and pulled out the letter. He opened it up and his face softened. He turned to Harli. "It's a birthday letter for Sophia."

Harli took the letter and looked at Alberto. "Why would your cousin have this letter?" she asked. "Does HE work for McGreggor?"

"I promise I do not know, senora," Alberto said. "I do not know who McGreggor is."

Harli sighed. "What do we do?" she asked Sanchez.

"He seems to be innocent to me," Sanchez replied. "But we need to find out who Andre is and how he is connected to Juan Carlos. We need to keep him here for a little while."

From behind them, they heard a soft voice whisper, "He is still alive. Gracias Dios." They turned around to see Angelica standing, holding her pregnant belly.

Sanchez gave her the letter. "It is for Sophia," he said gently. "For her birthday."

Angelica's eyes teared up. "He loves his family so," she said. "He even managed to get little Sophia a birthday note. But how?"

Harli responded, "We don't know yet, but we are about to find out. Everyone, back inside."

The crowd began to disperse, and Sanchez looked at Alberto. "If I take the handcuffs off, you won't try anything funny, will you?" he asked.

"Oh no, senor, not at all," Alberto promised. "I'm not a bad man."

Sanchez removed the cuffs and ushered him to the picnic table. "I really need to find out how your cousin knows Juan Carlos. You say you don't know who any of these people are, but I'm sure there is some information that you have that will be helpful. Think very hard, what does your cousin do for work?"

"I believe that he works at the sugar factory, senor," answered Alberto. "That is where he had me meet him."

Sanchez' eyes widened. "Harli!" he called. "Get over here!" Harli jogged over to the two men. Sanchez looked at her. "He thinks his cousin works at the sugar factory."

Harli gasped. "What? Then he DOES have a connection to McGreggor! That's where the truck was hidden."

"Exactly," said Sanchez. "I believe that it's possible Andre is one of McGreggor's lackeys. That would explain how he might know Juan Carlos."

Alberto looked scared. "I don't know anything about a truck either!"

"We believe you, Alberto," said Sanchez. "But your cousin might be mixed up with a very dangerous man. Juan Carlos, the man who wrote the letter, has been kidnapped. Did your cousin say anything, anything at all, that seemed weird or different?"

"Well, I have not talked to him in a long while," Alberto explained. "So, I was surprised that he called me to help him. All he said was that his friend had been detained, and it was important for the note to get to this village. And now that I think about it, he did say that it was also important for me not to be seen with him."

Once again, Harli and Sanchez exchanged looks. "Friend?" Harli asked.

"*Si,* he said *amigo,*" Alberto replied.

"That is weird," said Sanchez. "I wonder what he means by that. Alberto, I'm going to need his full name and address. And yours as well."

"Why, senor?" asked Alberto. "All he did was ask me to deliver a letter. I am not a criminal, and neither is he."

"You said yourself that you had not talked to him in quite a while," Harli said. "You don't know what he's been up to. Besides, when a detective asks you to do something, you do it!"

Alberto hung his head. "Alright," he consented.

Sanchez handed him a piece of paper and Alberto wrote down everything the detective needed. "No tricks?" asked Sanchez. Alberto shook his head no. "If you have lied to me, I will hunt you down. But for now, you are free to go."

Alberto ran to his truck and quickly drove away.

Harli looked at Sanchez. "This is great news!" she exclaimed.

"Yes," Sanchez agreed. "It is, but we still don't know if we will find out what we need to know. Do you want to go with me to question Andre tomorrow?"

Harli didn't have to think twice. "Absolutely!"

Sanchez stood up to leave. "Meet me at the coffee shop at nine o'clock. We'll go from there."

"Sounds like a great plan," Harli agreed. She stood up to walk Sanchez to his car. "See you tomorrow morning."

Harli slowly made her way back to the rest of the group, but she really didn't feel like celebrating. She needed some quiet time to write down the facts they had uncovered to this point. Just before she opened the door to the school, she changed directions. She went into the women's hut and dug out her notebook. She sat on her bed and began to write it all down. Maybe once she saw it on paper, it would start to make sense to her. She couldn't understand why this small piece of land was so important and why McGreggor wanted the villagers to leave their homes. This whole situation had her baffled. Especially the letter that was delivered from Juan Carlos. It was strange that a kidnapper would allow him to write and send a letter to his daughter. *This Andre guy must have a heart,* she thought.

Harli was startled awake by the sound of voices. "Oh, I must have dozed off."

"We wondered what happened to you," Jexi said. "I see you have your notebook. Are you making progress?"

"Yes, and no," Harli responded. We have gotten several leads but for the life of me, I can't figure out the motive behind it all. Yes, McGreggor wants the land. But why?"

"What if we dig up some information on McGreggor and the land he owns?" Shaya asked. "Maybe something will shake out in our research."

Aunt Jessie patted Shaya on the back. "That's a good idea, sugar. Let's get some rest and start first thing tomorrow."

"You girls are on your own for research tomorrow," Harli said. "I'm going with Detective Sanchez to find the guy who sent his cousin out here tonight with the letter for Sophia. He has to be connected to the kidnapping somehow."

"Whatever you need to do to get Juan Carlos back safely is the top priority," Jexi eagerly stated. "We'll keep our minds occupied with research. But first . . ." She put one finger in the air and pointed up for emphasis. "We sleep!"

"No," Shaya added. "First, we pray. Then we sleep."

CHAPTER TWENTY-ONE

The following morning was abuzz with activity. Harli was going to leave right after breakfast to meet Detective Sanchez at the coffee shop. Jexi and Shaya had plans to start their research but weren't sure exactly where to begin.

"We only have one vehicle," Jexi told the group. "We won't be able to go in different directions as we had hoped."

"Sure, we can," Harli said. You can just drop me off at the coffee shop because I'll be riding with Sebastian. He can bring me back later."

Jexi and Shaya both tossed questioning looks at Harli. "Sebastian?" they asked in unison.

Harli blushed. "I meant to say, Detective Sanchez."

"Oh my goodness! You like him!" Jexi exclaimed.

"Oh stop. We are just working together," Harli demanded. "Let's get going before we wind up being late."

Shaya giggled. "We can't be late to meet Sebastian!" Harli gave her a playful shove.

On the way to town, Shaya wrote down some questions they wanted to have answered. "We have some good ideas, but we don't really know what we are doing. We are not professionals like you, Harli."

Harli thought for a minute. "How about you go to the courthouse to talk to Manuel? See if he will tell you anything about McGreggor's land."

"Like what?" Jexi asked.

"Ask to see the paperwork about the land transfer. We know he got it when Henderson died, but we don't know the details of the transaction," Harli stated. Shaya quickly scribbled notes as Harli continued.

"Also, see if Manuel will look up the actual quantity and value of the land McGreggor owns. We also want to find out what his reason is for wanting this land so badly. Start there. That might give us some of the information we need."

Shaya stopped writing and looked at Harli. "Har, thank you for coming to help us. This means the world to Jexi. And to me."

Jexi spoke up. "She's right, Harli. We couldn't have done any of this without you."

Harli huffed. "You have Sanchez to help. I'm just doing what I can."

"You are the one who got us through to Sanchez!" Jexi said. "We were getting nowhere before you stepped in. Plus, you carry a gun, which makes us feel safe."

"I'm happy to help," Harli said. "These poor people are being taken advantage of and need others to stand up for them. I'm only doing what should be done. Besides, I like the villagers and despite everything, I'm having fun here."

Shaya giggled. "And you like Sebastian," she said in a singsong voice.

Harli blushed again and pointed at Shaya's notebook. "Back to the notes. Make sure to get as much as you can. Manuel might be hesitant to help at first, but he knows you and he was willing to get us that contract when we needed it."

The group arrived at the coffee shop and saw that Sanchez was already waiting. They walked in and sat with him in the booth. Immediately they began discussing their plans for the day.

"Do you know where we can use a laptop to look up some info?" Shaya asked Detective Sanchez.

"I have mine in the car," he replied. "You can use it. I won't need it for a while. They have Wi-Fi here in the coffee shop."

"Thank you," Jexi said.

Harli and Sanchez drove out to the address Bert, Andre's cousin, gave to them. Harli's mind was racing a mile a minute, but she was not able to put her thoughts into words.

"You are quiet," Sanchez observed.

"I don't know where to begin," Harli confessed. "I'm not used to being this flustered. Usually, I have it together when I interrogate a witness. This time feels different somehow. I guess it would be easier if I knew more of McGreggor's motive."

"I'm sure that Jexi and Shaya will get more about that today," Sanchez said. "And it's possible that we can get that from Andre."

The pair walked up the path to the house and a woman opened the front door with a young girl wrapped around her leg. Harli gasped and whispered, "He has a young family. I hope he isn't too deep into this mess."

"Hola. *¿Puedo ayudarte?"* the woman asked. "What is this?"

"Good morning, Senora Dominguez," said Sanchez, reaching out his hand. "I am Detective Sanchez with the Honduras Policia. This is my partner, Harli Chase. Is your husband home?"

Mrs. Dominguez took his hand and replied. "Delfini. Call me Delfini. What do you need with *mi esposo?"*

"I'm sorry, Delfini. I cannot say. Is he home?" Sanchez asked again.

"No, senor. He is working," Delfini stated.

"Where does he work," asked Harli.

"He works early shift at the sugar factory, senora," replied Delfini. "He will come home at four."

Harli's head snapped toward Sanchez. "Sugar factory?" she asked for clarification.

"Si," answered Delfini. "He is a hard worker, a good man."

Sanchez nodded, "I'm sure he is, senora, gracias. How long has he worked in the sugar factory?"

"He has been with them for almost ten *anos,* senor," Delfini said. "He wants to be in supervising soon." A small boy ran to the door and stopped suddenly when he saw Sanchez and Harli.

"Mama, Mama, who is this?" the child asked.

"This is Detective Sanchez and Harli Chase," Delfini told him.

"Are you in trouble, Mama?" he asked.

"Oh, no, *mijo,"* Delfini said. "They are just making sure we are all okay."

Harli kneeled to be at eye level with the boy. "Your mama has been very helpful," she told him. "What is your name?"

"I am Paulo. I am seven!" replied the boy. He pointed to the young girl. This is *mi hermana*, Elena. She is only four."

Harli extended her hand to shake Paulo's. "It is so nice to meet you, Paulo!" She turned to Elena. "And you too, Elena!" The girl smiled and shook Harli's hand. "We need to go now, but maybe we will see you again!"

Paulo looked disappointed. "You must go? Can you play with me? I have a badge, too!"

Sanchez looked at Harli who had stood back up. "I wish we could, buddy, but we need to go talk to someone else." He tousled Paulo's hair.

Sanchez looked at Delfini, "Do you talk to Andre during the day?" he asked her.

"Oh, no, senor," Delfini said. "I am unable to talk with him through the day. He work so hard and does not have time to talk."

"Gracias. Thank you for your time, senora," Sanchez said.

As soon as the doors closed on the car Harli squealed with excitement and surprise. "He is at the sugar factory. Is that our next stop?"

Sanchez nodded. "Yes, and we are going to talk to him now." He put the car in drive and drove away from the Dominguez home.

When they pulled into the parking lot of the factory, they saw two armed guards at the main entrance. They exchanged glances. "Why would a sugar factory need armed guards?" Harli asked.

"Good question," Sanchez replied. They exited the car and walked to the door. The guards stood in front of them.

One of them spoke. "How can we help you?" he asked.

Sanchez showed his badge. "We need to speak with Andre Dominguez, *por favor.*"

The guard spoke in Spanish into a walkie-talkie. Then he listened to the voice that answered. He turned to Sanchez. "Dominguez isn't here," he stated.

"Doesn't he work here?" Harli asked.

The guard spoke into the walkie-talkie once more and then looked at Harli. *"Si,* senora, he does."

Sanchez looked at Harli and stated, "Well, I guess we just have to get a warrant then."

The guard snapped to attention, "Wait, um, one moment, *por favor.*" He spoke into the device again. After he heard the reply, he looked at Sanchez. "Come with me," he said.

Harli and Sanchez followed him into the foyer of the building where a man in a suit was waiting for them.

"Hola, Detective," the man said as he held out his hand to shake Sanchez's hand. "I am Bruno Ortiz, the general manager. How can I help you today?"

"We need to speak with Andre Dominguez, *por favor,*" Sanchez said.

"Ah, yes," answered Bruno. "My guard mentioned that you were looking for him. I took the liberty to pull his file for you. As you can see, he is not here. He is on vacation." Bruno held the file out for them to see.

Sanchez reviewed the paperwork. "I see," he said. "Can we obtain a copy of this? I also would like to see the payroll records."

"Of course, senor," Bruno said. "I will talk with my secretary right away." He walked into the front office to address the young lady sitting there.

The girl opened the glass window partition. "Maddie will assist you with your request, Detective," Bruno stated. "Now if you will excuse me, I must attend to other matters."

"Certainly," Harli answered. "Gracias."

Maddie looked up at Harli and Sanchez. "You want payroll for Andre Dominguez?" she asked.

"Yes, please," Harli said. "And a copy of this work schedule showing that he is on vacation."

"I will help you," Maddie said. She took the paper and made a copy. She then looked in the file for payroll records. She pulled out a folder and opened it up. After shuffling through papers for a moment, she found the records for Andre. "Here they are," she said. She turned around and handed them to Sanchez.

Sanchez and Harli surveyed the information and then looked at each other again. "He's getting double vacation pay?" Sanchez asked.

Maddie took the file and read it. "Um, yes, it seems so," she answered. "But that is very unusual. Would you like me to call Senor Ortiz back?"

"No, thank you," Sanchez answered. "We will just take a copy of this."

After Maddie made the copy, Harli paused. "Double vacation pay is unusual, you say? Does that not happen very often?"

"No, not typically," Maddie answered. "Double vacation pay is only given when someone is working while on vacation. Most people don't choose that option. And as far as I know, Senor Dominguez hasn't been working."

CHAPTER TWENTY-TWO

Back at the courthouse, Shaya grabbed Jexi by the hand and said a quick prayer before entering the building. "Lord, guide us to the answers we need. Press upon Miguel to help us in any way he can. We trust you and know you have Juan Carlos in your hands. Help us to find him. In Jesus' Holy name, amen."

The two walked through the front door and past the security guards. Jexi kept her head down in case she was recognized from her previous visit. She didn't think it would be a big deal, but she couldn't be too careful.

Miguel was standing at his window assisting a customer when they caught his eye. He gave them a slight nod of acknowledgment. *"Buenos dias,* senoritas, I will be right with you as soon as I finish with this customer."

The lady in the booth next to Miguel's said, "I can help you here."

Miguel quickly interjected. "Gracias, Ana, but no. I have been helping them, and I will only be one minute." He looked at Shaya and Jexi. "You don't mind waiting, do you?"

Jexi shook her head. "Not at all, gracias."

Miguel quickly ended the transaction with his customer and the girls approached his booth. "Nice to see you again. How can I help you?" Miguel asked.

Jexi looked at their notes. "We need a few things, Miguel," she whispered. "Do you think you can get them for us?"

Miguel inconspicuously looked around. "Can I see what it is you need?" he asked. Jexi slid the paper to him, and he read the requests written there. "Let's step into a private office," Miguel suggested. He looked at Ana and said, "We are going to use the conference room for consultation and paperwork. It will take a few minutes. Will you cover my booth while I'm gone?"

Ana smiled. "Sure, Miguel!" she answered. Miguel put a closed sign in his window. He motioned to the girls to follow him to an office nearby.

Once inside the office, Miguel shut the door and took a deep breath. "What you are asking for is going to be hard to obtain," he said.

"But can you do it?" Shaya asked. "It would really help us out."

Miguel sighed. "Yes, I think I can. Here, fill out this paperwork. It is to apply for an international driver's license. This will make it look more official while I look for this information."

"Oh, thank you, Miguel," said Jexi. She and Shaya sat down at the table and began to complete the forms.

Miguel left and shut the door behind him. Jexi looked at Shaya. "What if he gets caught?" she whispered.

"He won't," Shaya said. "God has already placed Miguel at the courthouse for this purpose. And God's will always prevails."

Jexi relaxed her shoulders. "You're right," she assented, and she returned to the documents.

While the girls filled out the papers, Miguel set about the task of gathering the paperwork with the details of the land transfer between Henderson and McGreggor. After what felt like a lifetime, Miguel returned. "I have some good news and some not-so-good news. Locating the initial assessor's value of the land was easy." He handed the folder to Shaya. "This is what he actually paid for the property."

"What's the bad news? What about the land transfer?" Jexi asked.

"That's the strange part," Miguel said. "I found two different documents. They both have different information about how much McGreggor paid for the land. It also has a second assessor's report included."

Jexi looked at the pile of papers in front of her. She began reading the initial assessor's report. "It says here that the value of the land, all nine hundred acres, is fifty thousand dollars per acre. So, we know that is what McGreggor paid for the land, right?"

"That sounds right," Shaya said, "but look at this assessor's report. It says that the land is worth one hundred fifty thousand dollars per acre and that he owns one thousand acres."

"How can there be two different assessments?" asked Jexi.

Miguel spoke up. "I know what he did," he said. "He brought in a fake assessor."

The girls looked at Miguel with surprise. "He did what?" Jexi shrieked.

Shaya shook her arm. "Shh," she said. "Miguel, how do you know that's what he did?"

Miguel pointed to the signature on the original assessment report. "See that name there?" he asked. "I know this man. He works for the city." Then he pointed to the signature on the second assessment report. "That is not the same signature. It has been forged."

The girls examined the signatures side by side. They noticed the slight differences in the way that the names were scribed.

"You're right!" Shaya said. "But I don't understand. Forgery is illegal. Why does he need two different assessments? None of this makes sense."

Miguel replied. "McGreggor must have help, besides me, here at the courthouse. He could not have gotten a second report filed without someone knowing."

Jexi looked at Miguel. "Can you make copies of these for us, please?" she asked.

Miguel smiled. "I already did," he said as he handed an envelope to Jexi. "But I found something else interesting." He opened the folder and pulled out a document. "McGreggor also owns the sugar factory. I put this copy in your envelope as well."

Jexi's mouth dropped open. "Aha!" she exclaimed. "Wait till Sanchez and Harli hear this!"

Shaya shook her head. "This is all connected somehow," she said. She turned toward the court clerk. "Miguel, we are so grateful for your help," she said. "I am certain this was scary for you. It's probably best that you hide the original assessor's report, so it doesn't get destroyed."

"You're welcome, senorita," Miguel answered. "I will hide the document. It was a little scary, but I knew that I needed to do something. God told me that I would have to step up and help end this corruption. I am learning that it is always best to follow His will for my life."

Shaya and Jexi looked at each other. "We feel the same way, Miguel!" Jexi said. "Thank you so much for listening to Him. We appreciate you!"

The two girls rushed back to the coffee shop with copies of everything in their envelope. They were excited and nervous. They slid into a booth and began to review the papers.

"I can't wait to tell them!" Jexi exclaimed.

"Me too," Shaya answered. "For now, let's see what we can find on McGreggor with Sanchez's laptop." She pulled out the computer and linked it to the Wi-Fi. As the computer screen loaded, she looked at Jexi. "I sure hope they get back soon," she mused.

Almost immediately after she said that Sanchez and Harli walked in. Shaya breathed a sigh of relief as the two sat down in the booth next to them.

"What did you find out?" Harli asked anxiously.

"A lot!" Jexi answered. "But we have no idea what it all means!"

Shaya handed the papers to Sanchez. "This is good stuff!" she said. "McGreggor owns the sugar factory too!"

Harli attempted to snatch the papers from Sanchez. "What? Are you kidding?"

Sanchez tugged the papers out of her reach. "Hold on. Let me look at what we have."

Shaya continued. "He also has what we think is a fake assessment of the land. Miguel said that the signature was forged. Why would he have done that?"

Sanchez looked at the inflated assessment page after giving Harli the deed to the sugar factory. "Where is the original assessment report?"

"Here," Jexi said, as she handed him the other paper.

Sanchez nodded. "Yes, I know this man and this signature. He works for the city. This is definitely a forgery."

"So, how did your research go?" Shaya asked.

"One thing we know for sure is that the sugar factory is a key to the whole operation," Sanchez explained.

"Andre's wife said he was at work at the SUGAR FACTORY but when we went there to question him, the general manager informed us he was on vacation," Harli shared. "We have copies of his employee file, and it appears that he is getting paid double for his vacation."

"Wow!" exclaimed Jexi. "I feel like we are close to cracking the case!" When she noticed everyone giving her an odd look she added, "What? This is kind of fun. Sorry."

After they ordered lunch and ate, Shaya used the computer to search for Stan McGreggor. In a split second, there appeared to be page after page of information. "Yikes! This could take a while. We could use another computer."

"Let's go to my house," Sanchez suggested. "I have a desktop computer there. That way, we can accomplish more research."

CHAPTER TWENTY-THREE

Juan Carlos cautiously asked Andre if he was able to get Sophia's birthday letter to her. "I don't mean to be a bother. I just miss my family so much."

Andre turned to him. "I do not know, senor, but I am sure that it was delivered safely. I trust the person that I sent."

Juan Carlos sighed. "Okay, gracias, senor. *Dios lo bendiga.* God bless you."

Andre noted the sadness in the older man's voice. "Do not worry. Your little girl knows that you are thinking of her."

Juan Carlos looked up, surprised at the softness in Andre's tone. He smiled. "I am sure you are right," he responded. "God makes a way."

Andre looked around to ensure that they were alone. He leaned in close to Juan Carlos. "I have been thinking about this God of yours, old man," he said. "I listened to that sermon on the radio."

"Praise God!" Juan Carlos whispered. He turned around to talk with Andre. "You are not a bad man. Why are you working for a bad man?"

"I told you," Andre answered. "I need the money."

"There are more honest ways to earn a living," Juan Carlos replied. Don't you have a regular job?"

"I do have a job. But it doesn't pay this much," Andre answered.

"When you give your heart to God, that means you trust Him to meet your every need. It doesn't matter how much you make. He will provide just enough to take care of you and your family. I trust Him and He never lets me down."

Andre snorted, "Well, until you ended up in a basement jail cell, being held captive."

"God put me here, *mi* amigo," Juan Carlos answered.

"God put you in captivity?" Andre asked. "That doesn't sound like a very nice God."

"I assure you there is a reason. He put me here so I could meet you," Juan Carlos answered. "He wants you to know how much He loves you. That is why I am here."

Andre stared at Juan Carlos in disbelief. "He put you in jail so that you could meet me? How do you know?"

Juan Carlos smiled. *"Si,* so I could share the Good News with you also. It was the Lord's will that I be here so that you could be saved."

"I don't get you," Andre said. "You have been so nice to me, and I do not deserve your kindness."

"Dios gives me strength," Juan Carlos answered. "None of us deserves the kindness of the Lord and yet He showers us with it regularly. He wants you to experience it too. I'm glad you've been thinking about Him. Once you get to know Him, you will want more and more. Can I read some of my Bible to you?"

Andre hesitated. He was always worried that someone would come in and overhear their conversations. He didn't want to get into trouble for chatting with the prisoner. "Sure, maybe a little," he finally responded.

Juan Carlos began, "Let me read from First Peter, verses eight through eighteen. 'Finally, all of you, be like-minded, be sympathetic, love one another, be compassionate and humble. Do not repay evil with evil or insult with insult. On the contrary, repay evil with blessing, because to this you were called so that you may inherit a blessing. For, "Whoever would love life and see good days must keep their tongue from evil and their lips from deceitful speech. They must turn from evil and do good; they must seek peace and pursue it. For the eyes of the Lord are on the righteous and His ears are attentive to their prayer, but the face of the Lord is against those who do evil." Who is going to harm you if you are eager to do good? But even if you should suffer for what is right, you are blessed. "Do not fear their threats; do not be frightened." But in your hearts revere Christ as Lord. Always be prepared to give an answer to everyone who asks you to give the reason for the hope that you have. But do this with gentleness and respect, keeping a clear conscience, so that those who speak maliciously against your good behavior in Christ may be ashamed of their slander. For it is better, if it is God's will, to suffer for doing good than for doing evil. For Christ also suffered once for sins, the righteous for the unrighteous, to bring you to God. He was put to death in the body but made alive in the Spirit.'"

Andre let out a loud breath. "That is a lot of words, senor," he said. "What does that all mean?"

Juan Carlos was pleased that Andre was asking questions about God. He smiled. "The first part talks about being kind to others," he began. "It is necessary to always seek peace with all humanity. The second part talks about turning away from evil and doing good instead. Choosing to do the right thing may not always be easy, but it is worth it. Any suffering we experience is minor compared to what Jesus was put through. The final part says that it is more important to suffer for doing the correct thing than to suffer for making the wrong choice. Because if you are honest, you are suffering now, working for this man, are you not?"

Andre dipped his chin to his chest. When he finally looked back at Juan Carlos, he saw nothing but compassion on his face. "But what I am doing is not good or kind. I'm sorry for what is happening to you and your family. I wish I could make it right for you, but I don't see a way out. I don't see how I can turn from evil without putting my family in harm's way. My boss will stop at nothing to get what he wants."

Juan Carlos could see the conflict in Andre's eyes. "It will not be easy, amigo, but it can be done. Seek God's guidance and He will reveal the answer to you. Spend time in prayer and listening to the Lord. He will come to you and show you the way."

Andre looked at Juan Carlos with skepticism. "God will speak to me after all these things I've done?" he asked. "Besides, I do not know how to pray."

Juan Carlos smiled at Andre. "Praying is not hard to do. I will pray with you, and you can repeat after me. How you pray is not the matter, it is what you pray. God just wants to hear from you. Are you ready?"

"Right now?" Andre asked in disbelief. "I don't think I'm ready yet."

"Nonsense," replied Juan Carlos. "You are more than ready. Just repeat after me."

Both men bowed their heads, and Juan Carlos began. "Father God, I have sinned against You and others. Please forgive me." Andre repeated the words. "I have gotten myself into a situation and I do not know the way out." Once again, Andre spoke. "I am afraid for my and my family's safety, but I want to do the right thing. Please show me the way. In Jesus' name, amen."

Andre raised his head. "Is that it? That was really short."

"Prayer does not have to be complicated, Andre," Juan Carlos answered. "It just needs to be sincere, from the heart. Were those words sincere for you or do you need to say something else?"

Andre shook his head. "No," he answered. "That was exactly what I would have said."

"Then God will provide you with an answer, *mi* amigo," Juan Carlos said. "Just be patient and listen."

"You said to listen," Andre said, "but what am I listening for?"

"You will know it when you hear it," Juan Carlos said. "You will know that it is from the Lord. It is different from anything you have ever heard. It might not be a voice you can hear with your ears, but still, you will hear it. And do not stop praying."

The door to the basement opened and Andre's replacement walked into the room. "Shift change!" the short man announced.

"Pepe, you're late," Andre snapped. "Don't let it happen again."

Pepe looked at the ground. "Sorry, boss," he said. "It won't."

Juan Carlos winked at Andre as he left.

On the drive home, Andre repeated the prayer just as Juan Carlos had shown him. He wasn't sure why, but he believed God would hear him and help him. As Andre pulled into his driveway, he noticed that there was a strange car parked there. He parked on the street in front of his house and slowly got out of his car. He heard laughter coming out of the house, so he presumed that maybe his wife had a friend over.

When he walked into the house, he was shocked to see two very well-dressed people sitting on the couch and playing with his children. His wife had served iced drinks to them. The children stopped playing and ran to their father. "Papa!" they shrieked as they jumped into his arms. "The police are here!"

Andre stopped short in his tracks as he hugged his children and gently lowered them to the ground. He stared at the strangers and tried to speak. "W-w-welcome," he stuttered.

Delfini scolded him, "Andre," she said, "where are your manners?"

Andre cleared his throat. "Yes, of course. I am Andre. Pleased to meet you, officers."

Sanchez and Harli stood and moved forward to shake Andre's hand. "Actually, I am a detective, Sanchez, and this is an American private eye, Harli Chase. We would like to talk with you about your cousin, Alberto."

"Paulo, Elena, please go to your room," Andre said. After the children had scampered away, he continued. "Bert? Is he okay? What has happened?"

"He's fine," Harli answered. "But he happened to bring a note to Aldea Gracia the other day for a kidnapped man's daughter. He said that you sent him. What can you tell us about that?"

Delfini gasped in horror. "I assure you my husband knows nothing about a kidnapped man!"

Andre felt his face turn red. He tried to remind himself to stay calm. The words that Juan Carlos had said to him earlier came back into his mind. *Choosing to do the right thing may not always be easy, but it is worth it.* He felt a gentle nudge in his heart and heard a soft whisper say, *"Do the right thing."* He determined that this must be that voice Juan Carlos was talking about.

Andre turned to Delfini. "Can you give us a minute?" he asked her gently.

Delfini had a worried look on her face, but she obeyed Andre's request and went to check on the children.

Once she was out of earshot, Andre invited Sanchez and Harli to sit back down on the couch. "I want to talk to you, senor," he said softly. "But I will need protection for my family. I am less worried about myself, but my wife and children . . . " his voice trailed off.

"We will do our best to promise you safety," Sanchez started.

"No, senor," Andre interrupted. "You must promise that my wife and children will remain safe."

Harli placed her hand on Andre's forearm. She could sense the fear in this man, and she wanted to put him at ease however she could. "Tell us what you know," she urged quietly. "We will protect your family."

"Protect my family first," Andre demanded. "Then I will tell you everything I know."

CHAPTER TWENTY-FOUR

Aunt Jessie awoke with a gasp. She tried to make sense of the dream she had just had. In the dream, she saw the edge of the village and there were three trees near the river. The trees all had large ears and were leaning close to the ground, listening to the wind. The wind sounded disturbed and unsettling, but it was saying something. Jessie sat up on her cot quickly. It was almost as if she heard an audible voice say, *"Go now."*

Shaya heard Jessie's gasp and opened her eyes. "Aunt Jessie," she whispered. "Are you okay?"

"I'm not sure, child," Jessie answered. "I just had a dream, and I know that I am supposed to pay attention to it for some reason. It was not an ordinary dream."

"Let's step outside so we don't wake Jexi or Harli. We can talk out there, okay?" Shaya asked.

"I'm already awake," Jexi mumbled.

"Sorry, Jex," Shaya said.

"It's okay," Jexi replied. "I wasn't sleeping well anyhow. Something in me is just twisted tonight."

The three slipped on their shoes and walked out of the hut. They went to the picnic tables in the middle of the common area.

"Tell us what your dream was about," Shaya said to Jessie.

Jessie began, "There were three trees at the edge of the village, and they all had ears."

Jexi giggled. "Ears? On trees? What did you eat for dinner?"

"I know how silly it sounds," Jessie answered. "But it's important somehow. Anyway, they all leaned down to the ground near the river, and they were listening to the wind. There was something uncomfortable about the wind though, almost devilish. The trees were listening intently because they just had to know what the wind was saying. When I woke up, I felt like I heard God say, *'Go now.'*"

"We have to go to the edge of the village, near the river, don't we?" Shaya asked.

"Yes," Jexi answered. "And I think that we have to go right now."

Jessie nodded. "Both of you are right. Get jackets if you need them, but quickly."

The trio gathered jackets and flashlights and set off on their journey. There was silence between them as they walked gingerly. Mostly because no one really knew what to say, but also because of the trucks that drove around at night.

Once they reached the edge of the river, they looked around to see if anything looked familiar to Jessie.

"Are we in the right spot, Aunt Jessie?" asked Jexi. "I don't see three trees."

Shaya agreed. "I see trees, but not any three that are specifically together. And none of these trees have any ears!" she giggled.

Aunt Jessie gave Shaya a scolding look. "Don't mock God's imagery."

Jexi put her arm around Shaya. "We get it, Aunt Jessie, but you have to admit that it sounds a bit silly." "I know," Jessie admitted. "But I'm trying to figure this out too. So shush and listen."

All of a sudden, the girls heard the rumble of an engine from the darkness. "Get down!" Jexi whispered loudly. The three of them dropped to the ground into a prone position.

The truck pulled to a stop not far from the trio of women. Two men jumped out of the truck. "I am sick of riding in circles. How much longer are we going to have to scare these people?" said one male voice.

"Dude, for real! What's the point of showing off these guns if we aren't allowed to use them?" said a second voice. "Hold on, I gotta pee."

"Take your time," the first man said. "We have all night, and nothing is happening out here."

The second man returned from his break and addressed the other man. "I sure hope that McGreggor gets this deal done," he said. "This is boring. I want to see some action!"

The driver of the truck joined the other two men. "Guys, just shut up. This is what we were hired to do. Deal with it."

One of the men spoke up. "Man, Finn, we are just bored, is all. Can't McGreggor give us something else to do?"

The other man spoke. "Yeah, Felipe is right. Let's just go in there, eliminate them, and dump 'em somewhere. Nobody would miss them, and we'd be doing McGreggor a favor!"

Finn snarled, "Seriously, Javier, shut up already. You don't know what you're talking about. This is a very delicate situation and must be handled as such. Just because you're bored doesn't mean we do things your way."

Javier rolled his eyes. "Fine, *BOSS*, fill us in on what is so delicate about a bunch of loser villagers who won't move."

Finn shook his head. "This is on a need-to-know basis, and you already know what you need to know. That's it."

"He might not tell us what's going on, but I can tell you what I've heard," Felipe said. "McGreggor wants ALL this land, every bit. He's been telling a bunch of rich folks that he's growing sugarcane on the land. He gets them to invest in the land but he's not growing anything. He is selling stocks on the same plots of land multiple times and making a killing!"

Javier shrugged. "So why does he need the land anyway? If he's going to lie, he can just lie and say he owns it, and no one will know."

Felipe shrugged his shoulders. "Maybe he just doesn't want any interference."

"Shut up!" Finn demanded. "You both talk too much."

Felipe laughed. "Okay, boss, but I'll tell you one thing. I am going in with him so I can share some of those profits he is pulling from all those other suckers!"

"Dream on. He doesn't even know who you are," Javier said.

"Get back in the truck," Finn said. "We need to make another round."

"Fine, boss," Felipe said sarcastically as he rolled his eyes. "Another night of excitement."

Jessie's eyes grew large. She motioned to the others to lie still until the truck had moved out of sight.

As soon as it was safe to talk Jexi quietly squealed. "We were the trees!"

Jessie nodded. "Yes, we were! That is why God wanted us to go right away. Now we know what McGreggor is up to, and we can tell Harli in the morning. Now let's get back and get some rest before breakfast."

As the three were walking back, they chattered excitedly about what they had just overheard. "We should write this all down in the notebook while it is still fresh in our minds," Shaya told the others.

They were almost to their hut when they saw three shadows in the distance. They stopped in their tracks and shined their flashlights on the figures. "Who is that?" asked Aunt Jessie.

Hunter, Ben, and Harli ran to them from out of the shadows.

"Oh, thank goodness!" said Shaya. "You scared us to death!"

"What are you all doing out here in the middle of the night?" Ben asked. "Don't you know how unsafe it is?"

Hunter glanced at Jexi, and she could see the relief on his face. "We were worried about you! Harli woke up and you weren't there, so she came to get us."

"Where were you?" Harli asked frantically. "What are you doing out here so late? I was so scared that something had happened to you."

"There is so much we need to tell you, Harli," said Aunt Jessie. "But let's get back to the center of the village first. Then we can all sit down and talk."

The group walked the rest of the way to the picnic tables, and everyone sat down. Immediately, all three ladies started to speak at once.

"Whoa! Whoa!" exclaimed Harli. "One at a time, please!"

Jessie spoke up. "I had a dream, and it woke me up." She continued to share the details of the dream and how the three of them ended up by the river.

"Why didn't you wake me to go with you?" Harli interrupted. "I have a gun and could have protected you, in case you got into a jam."

Jessie looked Harli square in the eyes and replied, "There were only three trees. I didn't know what that meant at the time, but that is what it boils down to."

Harli scoffed. "Fine, tell us the rest," she said. Between Jessie, Jexi, and Shaya, the story of what the men had said about McGreggor unfolded. When they finished, Harli stared at them in shock. "This is all starting to fall into place."

"I hate to say this because we are all wound up," Shaya said. "But we really need to get some sleep. We are going to have a lot of things to do tomorrow."

"Starting with calling Sebastian," Harli interjected.

Shaya and Jexi giggled. "Ooh," they said in unison.

Harli shot them a glare. "Well, he does need to be informed of all this, doesn't he?" She stood up and turned toward their hut. "Goodnight."

"Wait," Jexi called. "Let's write everything down before we go to sleep. I don't want to forget any details."

CHAPTER TWENTY-FIVE

The next morning, after Andre had gone to work, Sanchez pulled up in front of his house. He needed to be careful, in case someone was watching. He would make this a formal visit at the front door, just to let Delfini know to pack some things for her and the children. He intended to keep his promise to Andre so that they could get Juan Carlos back to his family. He wasn't sure how he was going to get them out of the house to safety, but he would find a way. He made his way to the front door and knocked lightly.

Delfini opened the door a crack. "Oh, good morning, Officer. Won't you come in?"

"No, thank you. I will only be a moment," Sanchez told her. "Did your husband tell you our plan?"

"Si," Delfini answered.

"Good," Sanchez said. "Start packing for a few days away. Do not tell anyone you are leaving. Someone will be by to pick you up later today."

"Si, senor," Delfini responded. "We will be ready."

On the way back to his car, his cell phone rang. It was Harli. "Good morning," he said, as he connected.

"We need to meet right away," Harli rushed to say. "I have information."

"Coffee shop?" Sanchez asked. "In an hour?"

"Yes," Harli answered. "Can we make it thirty minutes? I'm already on my way."

"Sure can," Sanchez said. "I was just making sure Delfini was ready to go. I'll see you in thirty."

The two arrived at the coffee shop at the same time. Neither said a word until they were in their booth. "McGreggor is trying to run a scam," Harli said quietly. "He wants to sell land stocks to multiple investors. He is going to claim that he's growing sugarcane, but of course, that won't happen. He will pretend that the investors will make a substantial return on the money the phony sugarcane generates."

"This is huge! How did you get this information?" Sanchez asked.

"That is a strange and intriguing story," Harli said. "Jessie said she had a dream and that led her, Shaya, and Jexi out to the river in the middle of the night, where they overheard a couple of McGreggor's goons talking. That is the very condensed version."

Sanchez had a confused look on his face. "A dream?" he asked. "A dream led them to the river in the middle of the night?"

Harli nodded. "Yep, I know it sounds insane, and there are many more details, but it's all true—something to do with trees and ears. I'll let Jessie share the specifics. What is important to us right now is that we know McGreggor is up to no good and he needs to be stopped."

Sanchez sat silently for several minutes. "I wish they hadn't put themselves in danger like that but it's important information. Right now, it's just hearsay. We need a way to get proof."

"We told them the same thing," Harli said. "I wish they had taken me along for protection, but like you said it's good intel. As for proof, I have no idea of how to get it."

"Once we get Andre's family to safety, he will tell us what he knows," Sanchez said. "Hopefully, he will have the details we need."

"Speaking of Andre's family," Harli said. "Where are you taking them? How are you getting them out of the house unnoticed?"

"I haven't hammered out the deets yet," Sanchez replied. "I was hoping you might have some ideas."

"What if we use someone from the village?" Harli asked. "Maybe one of the elders could act as Delfini's mother. If she leaves with her 'mother' it won't look suspicious to anyone watching."

Sanchez considered for a moment. "Hmm, that could work. But we also need a safe house. We can't use any that are owned by the Honduran police. That is too risky."

"Would it be safe to take them to the village?" Harli asked.

"Not if McGreggor's men are still watching them," Sanchez replied. "I'm thinking of taking them to my house. I have a basement with plenty of room."

"That's risky," Harli noted.

"Yeah, but it's all I've got unless you have other ideas," Sanchez said.

"We really need to get them out of town," Harli said. "Like far out of reach. Choluteca even. What if I pay for a hotel as far away as we can get them from here?"

Sanchez looked at her in shock. "Are you serious? That is a very generous offer."

"I want them safe," Harli said. "And I want Juan Carlos home. I will do what is necessary to make those things happen."

"Well, I have to say that it's a good idea," Sanchez said. "It's feasible that Delfini's mother could live in another city. It would look convincing to others. Thank you, Harli. That is very kind." He reached out and placed his hand over hers.

Harli glanced at his hand on hers and slowly pulled back. "I'll reserve a hotel room and head back to the village to find someone to pick up the family. I think I know someone. Her name is Barrialina and she is very kind."

"Sounds like a good plan," Sanchez said. "Before you go, let's talk about Andre. We also need to get him to safety once he tells us what he knows."

"Won't it be suspicious if he doesn't go back to work?" Harli asked. "Maybe we should instruct him to keep working until we are ready to move in and take down McGreggor."

Sanchez paused. "You are probably right," he said. "I'm just ready to get him to safety as quickly as possible."

"Me too," Harli responded. "But if he does not return to work, there is a chance of them hurting Juan Carlos."

"Harli, I'm glad you are here," Sanchez said. "I'm usually better at thinking through potential problems but this case has me all messed up inside."

"I'm glad we're working together. We make a good team," Harli said. "Another thought about Andre. It might look better for him if we pretend to arrest him with everyone else. That way we don't blow his cover too soon."

"See," Sanchez said. "That's exactly why I'm glad you're here."

"When are we making the move?" Harli asked. "I need to know when to tell Barrialina to pick up the family."

"Midafternoon seems like a good time," said Sanchez. "Will that give you and Barrialina enough time? Delfini said she would be ready whenever we get there."

"If I leave right now, that should work," Harli answered. "We will have to obtain another vehicle; Ken and Sharon's van has been seen way too many times. I'll let you know what we figure out. Talk to you later." She stood up and walked out of the coffee shop to the van.

Back in the village, Harli called everyone together and explained the events that had taken place over the past several hours. She discussed the specifics of how Andre planned to help the police and that there was a plan in place to keep Andre's family safe. Immediately, JC stood up. "This Andre, he's the man that is holding my father captive?" he asked.

"He is one of them, yes," Harli said. "But he is not the man in charge of the whole operation."

"I don't care!" JC yelled angrily. "His family doesn't deserve protection. No one cared about my father's family when they took him! Why should we help this Andre person?"

"JC, I know you're angry, and I understand," Harli said gently. "But Andre has agreed to help us get your father back safely and also to bring down McGreggor with what he knows. We need his insider information. And if McGreggor finds out that he is working with us, his family will be in danger. We are doing whatever we need to do in order to bring your father home."

JC stewed for a moment. "I don't agree that this is what we should do," he said faintly. "What if Andre is leading us straight into a trap? What will happen to my father then?"

Angelica stood up next to JC and placed her arms around his shoulders. *"Mijo,* I know you are scared. We all are," she comforted. "But if this man will help us, we need to accept the help. Your father would want us to do this. God has given us an opportunity to be reunited as a family. *Dios* will see us through."

JC looked at her with tears in his eyes. "Mama, if you say that this is God's plan, then I will not get in the way." He sat back down.

Harli then shared the particulars of getting Andre's family to the hotel in Choluteca. She looked toward Barrialina. "Is this something you think you could do for us?" she asked. "Can you pick up Delfini and the children and drive them to Choluteca?"

Immediately Barrialina agreed. *"Si,* senora," she said. "I can do this. I will be happy to help my village."

Ben stood up. "Is that a good idea?" he asked. "To send Barrialina alone? Shouldn't it be one of us men?"

"I get your concern," Harli said to Ben. "But it really needs to look like Delfini's mother is picking her up and the kids for a trip. We need to make this as authentic as possible."

"I don't like putting my wife in danger," Ricky added. "But we need to do everything we can for Juan Carlos."

"What if we follow at a safe distance?" Jexi asked.

"Yes, definitely," Hunter said. "And not only that but does it just have to be Delfini's 'mother'? Couldn't it be her 'father' also? Ricky could pose as her father, and it would still look like Delfini visiting her family. That would increase the safety factor."

Harli pondered the suggestion. "Let me call Sanchez really quick to see what he says. I like the idea. Be right back." Harli stepped away from the group and hit the send icon when she found Sebastian's phone number.

"Are we all set?" Sanchez asked quickly.

"Mostly," Harli said. "But we have a snag. Barrialina's family isn't comfortable sending her alone. They want to know if we can send her husband with her. Does Delfini have a father?"

Sanchez responded with a deep sigh. "I hadn't even considered that. I don't know if she has a father so maybe anyone watching won't either. If that will make her family feel better, let's do it."

"Okay," Harli said. "Then I think we are all set and will head into town within the hour. We are going to borrow a car from the neighboring village. I'll call you when we get to town. I am going to follow them in the van."

"I don't think that's a good idea," said Sanchez.

"I will keep my distance. I'm pretty good at tailing," Harli said. "Why don't you ride along in the van with me?"

"Absolutely!" Sanchez exclaimed. "See you soon."

CHAPTER TWENTY-SIX

Harli and Sanchez rode in the van at a good distance behind Ricky, Barrialina, Delfini, and the kids. Despite the casual small talk being made between them, both were extremely nervous. Even while navigating traffic, Harli was scanning the area consistently for any possible danger. Sanchez's eyes were also busy, evaluating other cars and people for potential threats.

"Thanks for riding with me," Harli said to Sanchez.

"You're welcome," he replied. "I feel safer having us both watching over things."

Once they arrived at the hotel, Harli went inside to register and pay. Delfini and the kids stayed in the car, patiently waiting. Before long, Harli emerged with a room key and directed Ricky to pull behind the building.

"You are checked in as Harli Chase," Harli told Delfini. "Stay in your room, unless it is a dire emergency."

"We saw a grocery store on the way," Sanchez added. "Harli and I will go pick up enough food to last a few days. We don't know how long it will take to get you back home. We want you to be safe. Please don't contact anyone."

"Barrialina and Ricky will help you get settled," Harli said. "We will be back soon."

Once Sanchez and Harli had returned with groceries and some necessities, they repeated Delfini's instructions. "Please don't leave the room," Sanchez reminded them. "Right now, no one except us knows that you're here and we want to keep it that way. He handed Delfini another business card. "Here, I want to make sure you have my number. Call me if you need anything or if you see anything strange."

Delfini nodded. *"Si,* senor, gracias. Thank you for helping us. Please keep my husband safe, also."

"As long as he cooperates, we will protect him to the best of our ability," Harli said.

Later that day, Harli parked the van outside the Dominguez home. "The lights are on. He must be home," she said. "Let's see what he has to say."

"I really hope McGreggor's men aren't watching the house. Otherwise, they might get suspicious at our repeat visits," Sanchez said.

Harli pondered the comment. "I think McGreggor trusts him. At least I hope that's the case," she said.

No sooner had they knocked on the door, than Andre opened it and ushered them inside. "How is my family?" he asked anxiously. "Are they someplace safe? Where no one can get to them?"

"They are safe," Harli reassured him. "May we sit down, please?"

"Si, si, of course," Andre said. "Where did you take Delfini and the children?"

"The less you know, the better," Sanchez replied. "We promise you, they are okay. Now, let's talk. You agreed to tell us everything you know about McGreggor."

Andre sat down across from them and took a deep breath. "He had Juan Carlos kidnapped when the villagers refused to leave the area," he confessed. "I help guard him during the day. Delfini doesn't know; she thinks I am still going to the sugar factory. That is my regular job. I did not know I would be guarding a prisoner when I agreed to do work outside the factory." Andre buried his face in his hands. "Juan Carlos is safe. He is not being harmed. I am starting to think of him as an amigo."

Harli put her hand on his shoulder. "Thank you for deciding to help your friend."

Andre continued with his story. "McGreggor only wanted to scare the villagers into leaving their land. But I am afraid he will harm Juan Carlos if they still refuse to leave."

"Then we need to get him out of there as soon as possible," Sanchez said.

"McGreggor has men everywhere, senor," Andre protested. "But I may know a way to get him out without being seen."

"Really?" asked Harli. "Explain."

"I have been looking around before and after my shift," Andre said. "I found a tunnel that leads from the basement into the woods on the north edge of the property. There is a guard outside the tunnel. I can get Juan Carlos through the tunnel, but I don't know how to get past the guard."

"Is there ever a time when there isn't a guard outside of the tunnel? Like during a shift change or something?" asked Harli. "Or could the guard be distracted?"

"Wait," Sanchez said. "What if you took him a cup of coffee laced with a heavy dose of sleeping pills?"

"*Si.* I could do that before my shift," Andre responded. "From the outside. I don't want to give anyone a hint that I know about the tunnel. But what happens once we get into the woods from the tunnel?"

"We'll look around near the edge of the property to see if we can find an exit strategy," Sanchez said. "In the meantime, take the guard a coffee tomorrow to build trust. We won't lace this one."

Harli nodded. "Yeah, if he drinks it then there is a good chance our plan will work. But how are we going to get our hands on sleeping pills? And how do we know the right amount to put in the coffee? We want a good and deep sleep, but we sure don't want to kill him."

"I have some sleeping pills in the medicine cabinet," Andre offered. He stood up and walked out of the room. He returned quickly carrying a small white bottle. He handed it to Harli.

"We want him to sleep for a while because if he wakes up, he could go straight to McGreggor," Sanchez said. "I have a friend who works at a pharmacy. She can advise me on how much to put into the coffee."

Harli looked at Andre. "Are you sure you can do this?"

Andre looked up from the floor. *"Si,* I can," he replied.

Harli then turned to Sanchez. "Sounds like we have a plan then. Let's go talk to your friend at the pharmacy." She turned to Andre. "Can you meet us at the coffee shop in an hour? It might look suspicious if we keep coming back to the house."

"Right," agreed Sanchez. "But let's meet somewhere else. Delfini isn't home and I'm guessing you aren't much of a cook. Let's get you some dinner."

Andre laughed. "No, Senor. I do not cook."

"Neither do I," laughed the detective. "I know a good restaurant not far from here called Cafe Honore. Best tamales you've ever had. We'll meet there."

Andre and Sanchez shook hands. "Thank you, detective," Andre said. "But I'm sure you have never had my wife's tamales."

"You're welcome," responded Sanchez. "And while I'm sure Delfini's tamales are amazing, we have to make do with what we've got," he added with a laugh. "Thank you for helping us. We will see you soon."

On the way to the pharmacy, Harli questioned Sanchez. "You don't cook?" she asked. "How do you get fed?"

"I eat out a lot," Sanchez replied. "Or frozen meals. I do have meals with my mama a couple of times a week and she sends me home with lots of leftovers."

Harli laughed. "Sounds like you need a woman in your life, if there's not one already."

"I don't have any other woman cooking for me," Sanchez answered. "No woman for anything else either, for that matter."

Harli turned to look out the window so that he wouldn't see her blushing. A slight smile crept upon her face.

"What about you?" Sanchez surprised her with the question.

"I don't have a woman either," Harli replied laughing.

"You know what I meant," Sanchez quipped.

"Yeah, but that was funny, don't you think?" Harli asked. "But no, I am not in a relationship."

"Have you ever had a serious relationship?" Sanchez asked.

"Oh sure," Harli replied. "As a matter of fact, I was ready to marry one man until I discovered he was a narcissist. I decided I couldn't spend my life with him after all."

"Narcissist, I don't think I know that word," said Sanchez.

"A narcissist is a person who is all about themselves," explained Harli. "They are very selfish. No one else is important to them, no matter what they say. They also blame everyone else for their mistakes. They are exhausting."

Sanchez nodded in understanding. "I may have known a couple of people like that myself."

"What about you?" Harli asked. "Any past relationships?"

"I am married to my job," Sanchez said. "No woman can tolerate my long hours and dangerous situations."

"I'm sorry to hear that," Harli answered. "I'm sure you'll find the right woman someday."

There was silence in the car for the remainder of the trip. When they arrived at the pharmacy, Sanchez asked Harli to stay in the car.

"Why?" Harli asked. "I'm as deep into this investigation as you are."

"Well, the pharmacy tech has a bit of a crush on me," Sanchez admitted. "I sort of use that to my advantage to get information when I need it. If she sees me with you then . . ." his voice trailed.

"You are awful!" Harli exclaimed with laughter in her voice.

"I know," Sanchez said. "But sometimes detectives have to use all of their resources to get what they need."

"Go talk to your 'girlfriend,'" Harli teased. "I'll stay here."

"She's not my girlfriend," Sanchez said defensively.

"Oh, just go," Harli said. "I was giving you a hard time." Sanchez turned and walked into the pharmacy. Harli could see the girl he had mentioned run from behind the counter and throw her arms around him. She was surprised to feel a flicker of jealousy in her heart.

She then saw Sanchez gently remove the girl's arms from his body and glanced back quickly at Harli in the car. She saw him start talking to the pharmacy tech and presumed that he was asking about the sleeping pills. She pulled out her phone and tried to distract herself by calling Jessie.

"Hello!" Jessie answered. "How are things going?"

"Hi, Jessie," said Harli. "Things are progressing, but a little too slowly for my taste. But I know that investigations take time. We do have a plan, but I don't want to get anyone's hopes up, so I won't tell you much just yet. But I will say that we have an informant who works for McGreggor, and he is helping us."

"That is amazing!" Jessie replied. "Praise God! Does it look like we will be able to find Juan Carlos?"

"Yes, but please don't tell anyone else," Harli said. "Just in case the plan falls through." Harli paused. "I hate to ask, but is there any way you guys can research the land boundaries for McGreggor's home property?"

"Sure," said Jessie. "What are we looking for?"

"We were told that there are woods near his house," Harli replied. "I need to know exactly where that wooded area is and if it backs up to any main roads."

"Okaaay," Jessie said. "And?"

"That's all," Harli said. "I just need to know how to find the wooded area from outside the property."

Jessie sighed. "He owns a lot of land. I'm sure there will be several wooded areas."

"Look on the north side," Harli added.

As she hung up the phone, Sanchez walked out of the pharmacy and got into the driver's seat.

"I thought you said she had a LITTLE crush on you," joked Harli. "From what I saw, she is basically in love with you!"

Sanchez rolled his eyes. "Yeah, I guess she does have a thing for me. But I really am not interested. She's too young and probably too fragile to be a detective's wife. Besides, let's get back on track. I know how many sleeping pills to put in the coffee."

CHAPTER TWENTY-SEVEN

As soon as Jessie got off the phone with Harli, she went to find Jexi, Shaya, Hunter, and Ben. She wanted to use a tablet to look up the real estate boundaries for McGreggor's land. She located the group at the schoolhouse.

"Hey guys, can I use a tablet?" she asked them. "I need to look something up for Harli."

"Sure," said Shaya as she handed her tablet to Jessie. "What are you looking for?"

"Harli wants to know about the property lines of McGreggor's property. She asked if I could find any wooded areas to the north of it." "I wonder why she needs that," Jexi pondered.

"I don't know," said Jessie as she typed into the tablet. "She didn't say."

Jexi pulled out her tablet also. "I can help look too," she offered. Jessie nodded but didn't say anything.

Several minutes passed as the search continued. Jessie looked at one tablet while Ben and Shaya looked over her shoulder. Hunter looked with Jexi on her tablet, but no one was able to locate exactly what they needed.

"I can't find anything specific," Jexi said after several moments. "I can see some of the properties he owns, but no boundary lines."

"Me neither," said Jessie with disappointment in her voice.

"Let's call Miguel," Shaya suggested.

"Who?" Jessie asked.

"Miguel," Shaya replied. "The man at the courthouse that helped us. Maybe he will be willing to help us again."

Ben put his arm around Shaya's shoulder. "My wife is so smart!" he said.

Jexi giggled. "Shaya is right. Miguel was overly helpful last time. He seems like he wants to do what's right. I'm sure he will help us again."

Hunter's face clouded with concern. "But the guards and everyone at the courthouse have seen all of us. Will it be safe to go in again?"

Jexi nodded. "Of course!" she said. "The last time, he made it look like we were filling out international driver papers. We can just act like we had a problem with them and need more help."

Hunter scowled. "I still don't like it," he protested. "I worry that if you go back, you will be in danger. Can we think of another idea?"

"I'll go," Jessie suggested. "Nobody at the courthouse has seen me."

Jexi quickly added, "I will call Miguel and let him know you are coming first thing tomorrow morning."

Hunter eased. "I think that's a better plan," he said.

Jexi looked at him. "You are really worried about us, aren't you?" she asked.

"Um, yes," Hunter said. "This is a very serious matter with very dangerous men. They've already shown us what they can do to get what they want. Why wouldn't I be worried?"

"But the men we heard last night said they weren't allowed to use their guns," Shaya stated.

Ben took Shaya's hand. "I know what you heard, but we are sure that these men are capable of much more. We don't want either of you to get hurt. We don't want Jessie or anyone else to get hurt. It's natural for us to worry."

"I have an idea," Jexi said. "Why don't we all ride into town with Jessie tomorrow and have breakfast? We haven't done much outside of the village since we got here."

"That's brilliant!" Hunter exclaimed. "Then Ben and I can be there to help keep you all safe."

"Oh, yes, Hunter," Jexi said sarcastically. "You must protect the little women who can't protect themselves."

Shaya sensed the offended tone in her friend's voice and changed the subject. "Did Harli say when she would be back? I can't wait to hear what happened today."

"No, she didn't say, but I think she'll be late tonight. She mentioned that they were still out investigating when she called," Jessie said.

"I'm so glad she decided to come," Jexi said. "She has been a great help."

Shaya smiled. "Yes, she has. She is an answer to prayer for sure."

Hunter nudged Jexi. "Um, can I talk to you for a minute?" he whispered.

Jexi nodded and the pair walked outside. She noticed that he seemed more fidgety than usual, so she tried to reassure him. "We will all be okay tomorrow," she said. "I am sorry that I snapped at you. I do feel safer knowing that you'll be there."

Hunter swallowed and took a deep breath. "Um, that's, that's not it," he said nervously. "Would you take a walk with me?"

"Now?" she asked. "We are in the middle of a big discussion with the others."

"Yeah," Hunter said. "We've already made a plan and all you need to do is call Miguel."

Jexi pulled her phone out of her back pocket. "Oh, right! Lemme call him really quick." She found Miguel's number and dialed. After a short conversation, she hung up. "We are all set for tomorrow," she said. "I guess we can go for that walk. Let me tell the others." She opened the door to the school and hollered in at the group. "Hunter and I are going for a walk. We'll be back for dinner."

As the door closed, Ben said under his breath, "No you won't."

"Let's go closer to the river," Hunter suggested. "It's such nice scenery there."

The two walked toward the river but little was said. Hunter reached for Jexi's hand, and she did not pull away. She could feel the butterflies in her stomach the moment his hand made contact with hers. She also felt warmth and peace.

Within moments, she could hear the dulcet tunes of a makeshift guitar. She glanced at Hunter who had a smile on his face. "Someone is playing by the river," she said. "And it sounds lovely." She tugged on his hand as she quickened her pace. When they reached the riverbank, she gasped. "What is all this?"

"I set up a picnic dinner for us," he confessed. "Diego and Dante agreed to play the guitars that we made for them."

"They have learned so much!" Jexi exclaimed. "You are an amazing teacher!" Jexi then looked and saw a blanket with a picnic basket sitting on it. Next to the basket was a bouquet of fresh wildflowers. She gasped. "Oh my, it's beautiful! When did you have time to do all this?"

"All what?" Hunter asked. "It was really no big deal."

"No big deal?" Jexi asked. "It's very special! No one has ever done anything like this for me."

Hunter turned toward her and took both of her hands in his. "You are very special," he said as he helped her down to the blanket. The boys continued to play as Hunter began to unload the basket. Jexi took it all in. She noticed there were unlit lanterns on all four corners of the blanket. Hunter took out a match and lit all of them; a soft glow filled their space. Jexi felt as if there were no one else in the world.

"Hunter?" Jexi started and then stopped.

"Hmm?" Hunter asked as he turned around and sat down.

"Nothing," Jexi said.

"Are you okay?" asked Hunter. "Should I not have done this?"

Jexi looked at him. "No, that's not it," she said, "This is incredible. I am glad that you set this up. But I guess I just want to know . . . why."

"Jexi," Hunter said, "You know why."

"I do?" she asked.

Hunter nodded. "I've been trying to tell you for a while now. I care about you. I have feelings for you and have since I first met you. I have prayed and prayed, and God keeps telling me that you are the one."

Jexi's hand flew to her mouth and her eyes went wide. "Hunter!" she exclaimed.

"I'm not saying we need to run off and get married tonight or any- thing," Hunter joked. "But I would like for us to explore the possibil- ity of a relationship."

Jexi's eyes then filled with tears. She had never felt this way about anyone, even Brennan. She leaned over and gave Hunter a kiss on the cheek. "I'd like that," she whispered.

They embraced each other in a hug and the world stood still. The stress and worry of their situation temporarily evaporated. The soft guitar music and gentle glow of the lanterns created a perfect setting for them to make their relationship official. Jexi felt like her heart would explode with happiness.

The guitar music stopped abruptly, and both boys yipped with ex- citement. "It worked!" Dante yelled.

"I guess I don't get to marry you after all," Diego joked.

Hunter and Jexi laughed. They had virtually forgotten about the boys. "Thanks, guys," he said. "I am grateful for your help. You can go back to the village now."

Dante snapped his fingers. "Oh bummer, we don't get to stay?"

"Not this time," Hunter answered. "Thanks again." The boys start- ed the walk back to their house.

"Will you let the others know we won't be back for dinner?" Jexi asked.

Hunter grinned. "They already know," he said slyly.

Jexi playfully slapped him on the arm. "Sneaky!" she said.

"I didn't want them to worry," Hunter explained. "So, I told Ben and Shaya."

Jexi laughed. "It figures that they would know. And it figures that Shaya kept such a great secret! But I'm grateful. This has been a wonderful night."

"It's not over," Hunter said. "We still have some delicious dinner!"

"I just have one more thing," said Jexi.

"Shoot," Hunter said.

"Thank you for waiting for me," she said. "I know I didn't make it easy. I just wasn't ready."

"But you are now?" Hunter asked.

"Yes," Jexi answered. "I'm more than ready."

Hunter leaned in and kissed her softly. "You are worth waiting for!" he whispered.

Jexi wiped the tears from her eyes. "Let's get to that food!" she said. "I'm so hungry!"

"Wait," Hunter said. He reached for her hand. "Let's pray." Jexi bowed her head with him. "Heavenly Father, we come to You together, as an official couple, to thank You for everything You have done for us. We want to do Your will in our lives and will follow where You lead. Please show Your favor to this village and its people because they made it possible for us to finally find our way to each other." Jexi smiled at his words. "Lord, we love You and will always show Your love to one another." Hunter paused and then added, "In Jesus' name we pray, amen."

"Amen," Jexi added.

CHAPTER TWENTY-EIGHT

The next morning at Rosa's Diner, the group ate breakfast. Harli and Sanchez decided to join them since they needed to eat as well, and they really needed to talk about the case. After Jessie had eaten, she prepared to go to the courthouse.

"Miguel said he would pull the property maps as soon as he got to work," Jexi said. "You just need to tell him your name and that you have an appointment with him."

Jessie inhaled and exhaled deeply. "Got it," she said. "I'll be back soon."

"Keep your cell phone on," said Sanchez. "Text us if something feels off."

Jessie nodded and walked out of the diner toward the courthouse. Watching her walk away, Shaya said a silent prayer of protection over her.

"Okay, here's the plan," Harli said. "Most of you don't know this, but we know where Juan Carlos is being held."

Several gasps and exclamations of shock came from the group. They all started talking at once, demanding more information.

Jexi quieted the group as best she could. "Harli, Just tell us where he is and we will go get him! Better yet why aren't the police there getting him now?"

Harli shook her head. "It isn't that easy. Our informant, Andre, who works for McGreggor, is willing to help us bust Juan Carlos out. However, we have to be careful. We already know that McGreggor has a lot of the police in his pocket. He also has guys everywhere and we need to play it safe."

"Play it safe?" Shaya asked. "He is being held captive! He's in danger! What if they are hurting or torturing him?!"

Sanchez held up his hand to have Shaya stop. "Andre informs us that he is not being harmed. Yet. This is why we need to move quickly. Andre is going to befriend the man who guards the exit of the tunnel in the basement. He's going to take him coffee for two days. On the third day, we will lace it with sleeping pills. Once he falls asleep, we will go in and extricate Juan Carlos."

"That is why we need those maps," Harli said. "When we get them, we need to plot a route of escape. We are told that there are woods to the north and west of McGreggor's property and that we can possibly escape through there. The map will show us if a road connects with those woods so that we can get back. Sanchez and I are going to go out and look at the woods to make sure there is a way out to that road."

Jexi looked at Harli. "That sounds like a good plan. But why didn't you tell us sooner that you know where he is?"

"I couldn't promise you anything except that we knew his location," Harli explained. "I couldn't tell you that we had a plan or what would happen next. I also didn't want anyone doing anything rash, like running in there and getting hurt or captured. Waiting to tell you was best, but I'm sorry that it makes it seem like I was keeping secrets."

Shaya nodded. "We understand," she said. "What can we do?"

"None of us can do anything until we get the maps," Sanchez said. "Then we can plan our escape route. After that, we will wait for two days. That's all any of us can do."

"Angelica will be happy to have him home," Jexi said.

"He won't be going home right away," said Sanchez. "We can't risk him being seen by McGreggor's men and that will be the first place they look. We will take him to the hotel in Choluteca."

"Once we get Juan Carlos out of captivity, how are we going to take down McGreggor?" Hunter asked.

"That's the hard part," Sanchez said. "We don't know who we can trust. We don't know who we can take this information to."

"Wait," said Harli, "I have been a PI for a long time. I know some FBI agents. Since McGreggor has his main citizenship in the States, maybe he can get convicted there too."

"That might work," Sanchez said. "Good thinking, Harli. But we still have the issue of his arrest here."

"Yeah, we don't know how it will all work out, but we can cross that bridge when we get to it," said Harli. "In the meantime, we need to get Juan Carlos to safety. I'll give my contacts a call later today and see what I can find out from them."

Jessie walked back into the diner with a smile on her face. She sat down with the group.

"Well," Ben asked, "did you get them?"

"Yep!" said Jessie. "Took pictures of every single one." She pulled out her cell phone and opened the gallery app. There were the layouts of McGreggor's house and land and the property surrounding it.

"Can we get these printed out somewhere?" asked Jexi.

Sanchez spoke up. "Email those pictures to me and I'll print them at home. I live close so it won't take me very long. Stay put."

Jessie sent the pictures to him, and he opened his phone to verify they had come through clearly. When he was satisfied, he reminded the group to stay where they were, and he went to his car.

Meanwhile, Andre arrived at the McGreggor compound with two coffees in his hands. "Hey, Ron."

"Morning, boss," Ron replied.

"Thought you might like some coffee," Andre said as he held out one of the cups.

"Thanks, man," said Ron. "I really would. I am exhausted."

"No problem," said Andre. "I need you to be alert on the job. I've been getting reports that those villagers seem to be getting restless. No telling what they might do."

Ron scoffed. "They don't know anything about where this guy is being held so we don't have anything to worry about."

"No, they don't know, but we still need to be diligent and observant. Never know what could happen. I know how boring it is out here by yourself. Can't have you falling asleep on your shift."

"Sure, boss, sure," Ron reassured. "I won't let you down."

Andre turned to walk into the basement through the front door. When he got down there, he saw Juan Carlos reading his Bible. He dismissed the overnight guard and sat down. Once he was sure that the guard was gone, he turned to talk to Juan Carlos.

"I've been talking to the police," he said quietly. "I am working with them to get you out of here."

Juan Carlos threw his hands in the air and exclaimed, "Gracias, Jesus!" Then he looked at Andre. *"Por que,* senor? *Por que?* I am grateful, no doubt, but what has changed your mind?"

Andre sighed. "You got to me, old man. I told you that I listened to that sermon with you. I accepted Jesus as my Lord. He told me that I was helping the wrong man and that I must help you."

"Praise *Dios!"* Juan Carlos yelled as he clapped his hands.

Andre put up his hands to signal Juan Carlos to stop. "Pipe down. We don't want anyone to hear you. We have to play it cool for a couple of days."

Juan Carlos stopped clapping and smiled. *"Si,* senor, *si.* I will do as you say. Oh, *Dios,* gracias! You are so good to me!"

Andre filled Juan Carlos in on the plan to take coffees to Ron and then put sleeping pills in one of them.

"He won't die, will he?" asked Juan Carlos.

"No, no, it will just put him to sleep for a while," Andre said. He then relayed the rest of the plan to escape through the woods, find the road, and get Juan Carlos to the hotel in Choluteca.

Juan Carlos paused and then asked, "Wait, senor, if I disappear on your shift, that will make it look like you had something to do with it. You will get into trouble. Certainly, there can be a better way?"

Andre sat up straight. "You're right. That does pose a problem. I hadn't even considered that. I was so focused on getting you out of here, I wasn't thinking about myself. I will call Detective Sanchez and mention that. Thank you for thinking of me."

"Oh, you are welcome, *mi* amigo," Juan Carlos responded. "I don't want anything bad to happen to you after you are helping me. Let's try to think of a different plan."

After thinking and discussing options for several hours, Andre stepped out to call Detective Sanchez. They discussed the problem and agreed to come up with a different idea. Andre mentioned the idea of having the villagers create a false emergency during the night to distract the guards from their posts.

"That's great, Andre!" said Sanchez. "I will work with Harli on the specifics. I'll call you back soon."

Sanchez had returned to the diner with the pictures he printed. Before he handed them to the group, he informed them that there was a snag in the plan.

Harli thought for a while and then said, "He can drug the night tunnel guard since that is the best time for a distraction. When an emergency happens, the cell guard will leave to go help with that. That is when we'll make our move. Andre already told us that the keys to the cell are on a hook across the room. One of us will go in and get Juan Carlos and head to the woods."

"And Andre can help the security team with the fake emergency, so he is accounted for the whole time," realized Sanchez.

"Right," said Harli. "The fault will lie upon the night guards so Andre won't get into trouble."

"Who specifically will create the fake emergency though?" asked Ben. "And what kind of emergency would it be?"

"This is getting complicated," Shaya added. "I liked the simple plan better."

"Yes, it is," Harli said. "But plans like this often are. We have to think of every contingency. As far as the emergency, I'm thinking a fire. We can have a few of the villagers set some fires on the perimeter of the house property. The kind of fire that will burn for a while but eventually die out on its own. It won't spread but it will fool the guards into thinking that it might."

"But will the villagers be at risk if they set fires on McGreggor's property?" Jessie asked. "He seems like the kind of guy who would retaliate. I don't want anyone getting hurt."

Sanchez shook his head. "Jessie, I understand your concern. But we can use some explosives with a timer. Whoever plants the explosives can set the timer for two hours and be long gone before they explode. While the guards are extinguishing the fires, that will give someone time to get Juan Carlos out. McGreggor might want to retaliate, true. But he won't be able to prove that it was the villagers. And I doubt that he would harm someone if he didn't have proof."

"Okay," said Harli, "we have a plan. Now all we need to do is plot that escape route. Sanchez, where are those pictures you printed?"

"Right here," Sanchez said as he dug into his briefcase. He set the pages on the table. Harli took the one that had a view of the entire property.

"We will take advantage of these woods here to the north of the house," Harli pointed to the paper. "The tunnel comes out of the north side, so that's beneficial. It means we will spend less time out in the open. We will go straight from the tunnel to the woods."

Jexi pointed to an open area on the edge of the woods. "Is this a road? It's hard to tell."

"Yes," Sanchez said. "One of us will have the car there, waiting. We'll then take that road to get to Choluteca."

"It looks like the wooded area isn't too wide," Ben added. "It shouldn't take long to get him out."

"No," Sanchez said. "But they are dense. So, whoever is going through there needs to be careful. One more thing we need to address is the flashlight issue. We can't use them because they emit too much light."

"What about a rope?" Shaya asked.

"What do you mean?" questioned Harli.

"Well, we have to wait two days anyhow, some of us can put a rope through the woods with the end poking out of the woods, straight across the yard from the tunnel. Whoever gets Juan Carlos can use the rope as a guide through the woods until they get to the road."

"That could work," Hunter agreed. "They can take the rope with them, so it won't be discovered."

"How will they put the rope out without being seen?" asked Ben.

"Very carefully," replied Harli. "And quietly. Hopefully, the guard will just think it's a wild animal."

"Can we time it to when Andre is delivering coffee?" Hunter queried. "That way Andre's conversation can distract him."

"That's perfect," Sanchez said. "I feel good about our plan. This is going to work."

CHAPTER TWENTY-NINE

Back at the village, a small group gathered in the schoolhouse. Harli and Sanchez stood at the front and outlined the plan to rescue Juan Carlos.

"We need to determine who will be assigned to which steps," Harli said. "Sanchez and I are the ones who will get Juan Carlos to safety. We will also set out the rope ahead of time. We need a driver who can be ready as soon as we all get loaded. We will go straight to Choluteca."

Jessie stood up. "I'll do it. I'll drive y'all to the hotel."

"Thank you, Jessie," said Harli. She turned to the whiteboard and drew a quick sketch of the property layout. "Okay, now, we need two people to plant the explosives and set the timers." She marked spots on her drawing for the location of the drop-off, pickup, and explosive locations. "Someone will drop those two people off on the west side of the house and pick them up on the northeast side of the house."

"Antonio and I will set the explosives," said JC.

"I will teach you how to set everything up and start the timers," said Sanchez.

"Hunter and I will drive the car for the boys," said Ben.

"Got it," said Harli.

"What can we do?" asked Jexi.

Sanchez looked at her with just a hint of a smile. "Pray," he said. "We need this to go off without a hitch."

JC stood up and looked at everyone in the room. He cleared his throat before speaking. "Gracias to everyone for helping to get my papa free. This is dangerous for all of us, but I am thankful that you are willing to put yourselves in harm's way to get him home."

Jexi put her hand on JC's shoulder. "We love you," she said. Tears welled up in her eyes. "We love all of you."

Jessie interrupted the moment to say, "Let's all pray right now." Everyone in the room bowed their heads. Jessie continued. "Father God, we love You so much. We are humbled by how much You love us. Without You, we can accomplish nothing, but with You, all things are possible. We ask You to please guide our mission to rescue Juan Carlos, make it successful, and keep us all safe. Please show us the way to defeat the evil that has penetrated this area. We thank You for the way You have worked in the hearts of others. We thank You for Your blessings. In Jesus' mighty and powerful name, amen."

The group repeated a collective *"amen"* before dispersing to their cabins.

As they walked across the common area, Hunter reached for Jexi's hand. "Are you nervous?" he asked.

"Yes," Jexi replied. "But I have learned to put my faith in God. I believe this will all work out."

"I have to be honest," Hunter said. "I am also nervous. I've always been able to trust God, and I have no doubt that I can trust Him again. But there is much more at stake this time."

"What do you mean?" Jexi asked.

"I have you now," Hunter said. "I just found you and we have big plans when we return home. I don't want to lose you."

"You didn't just find me," Jexi said. "We've known each other for a while. But I understand what you are saying. I feel the same way." The two embraced each other.

"What do we have here?" Shaya asked as she and Ben approached the couple. "Looks like we need to talk, Jexi," she said with a wink.

Jexi blushed as she stepped away from Hunter. "Yeah, I guess we do. But don't pretend you don't already know. I am aware of your secret-keeping."

Hunter smiled. "You two go talk. I'm going to make sure that the car and van are gassed up and ready to go. I'll talk to you later." He leaned over and kissed Jexi on the cheek.

"Ooh," said Shaya giggling.

"Don't make it weird," Jexi said as she playfully punched Shaya in the arm.

Ben and Hunter walked away to go check on the status of the vehicles and the girls walked back to the hut. Once inside, Jexi sat down on her cot.

"So, spill already," said Shaya.

"There's nothing to spill, since you have been in on this from the start evidently," Jexi said. "Hunter and I went for a picnic dinner."

"Now you sound like me!" Shaya spat. "Come on, tell me what he said to swoon you."

Jexi laughed. "I learned from the best!" she said. "There was no swooning, alright? He just mentioned that he's had some feelings for me for a while and wanted to know if I felt the same."

"Geez-Louise, Betsy," Shaya said with a laugh. "That is the most boring romance story I have ever heard."

"Okay, okay," Jexi said. "He had a blanket laid out with lanterns on each corner. When he lit them, the light danced all over the area. It was beautiful. The boys were playing on their new guitars, and it was so sweet. I asked Hunter why he was doing all of this, and he said I already knew why. That he's had feelings for me since we met. He even said that he's been praying, and he's convinced that God told him that I'm the one! He wants us to be together. It was *VERY* romantic."

Shaya smacked her hands together and rubbed them back and forth vigorously. "Now we're talking!" she said. "Keep going!"

"That's it," Jexi said. "We were hungry, so we ate and talked and now here we are."

"No, that's NOT it," Shaya said. "What did you say in response? Are you together or not?"

Jexi smiled, "Didn't you see us out there, all snuggled up?" she asked. Then she looked at the ground and surrendered to her friend's inquiry. "Yes, we are. I said yes."

Shaya jumped up and down and squealed. "I knew it!" she yelled. Jexi couldn't help but join her. They laughed and danced around together for a minute. Jexi felt happier than she had in the longest time.

All of a sudden, they heard, "What in tarnation is happening in here?"

They whirled around to see Jessie standing in the doorway of the hut.

Shaya ran to Jessie, "Jexi and Hunter are officially a couple! It's about time, right?"

Jessie laughed. "I've known for a long time. I knew God's will would bring them together. I'm glad to see that they finally caught up!"

All three laughed and Jexi regaled Jessie with the story of Hunter's picnic dinner. It was nice to have a bright spot in the midst of the madness. Jessie prayed aloud and thanked God for always giving them something to be happy about.

That evening, the village sat around the tables in the common area eating a hearty and delicious meal. There were shouts of praise and thanksgiving to God and smiles on all the faces. All that remained now was waiting for the day after next to implement the daring rescue.

Harli's phone rang, interrupting their celebration. "I need to get this. It's my FBI contact," she said quickly. She took a few steps away from the crowd and said, "Frank, hello! Thank you for calling me back. I need your help."

"What can I do for you, Harli?" Frank asked. "Your message mentioned that you're in Honduras?"

"Yes, I am," she answered. "I'm helping a friend on a kidnapping case. We've figured out all the details and we know a man named Stan McGreggor is behind it. We need help because he's not only kidnapped someone, but he's also selling phony land stocks. I can get you all the info we have, but do you think you can help?"

Frank cleared his throat. *"McGreggor? Is that the name you said? Stan McGreggor?"*

"Yeah," Harli said. "Why?"

"That name rings a bell," Frank replied. "Hang on a sec. I'm opening my computer now."

After a couple of quiet moments, Frank addressed her. "Harli, be careful. I found out why that name was familiar. McGreggor is bad news. We've been surveilling him for a while. It doesn't surprise me that you're saying he's involved with a kidnapping."

"Why would you be surveilling him if he is in Honduras?" Harli asked.

"That's the thing," Frank said. "He's not in Honduras. He's here in the States. I shouldn't be telling you this, but I know I can trust you. He's suspected of running a drug ring from Honduras to the States using a sugar factory as a cover."

Harli was quiet for a moment as she processed what he was saying. "DRUGS?" she finally asked in disgust. "You have got to be kidding me!"

"Cocaine, specifically," Frank replied. "And we know that there probably isn't anything he won't do to protect himself. That's why you need to be careful. You're deeper than you know."

"Back up a minute," Harli requested. "He isn't even here? Who is doing his dirty work in Honduras?"

"Probably his second in command," answered Frank. "Man by the name of Holland. Just as nasty as McGreggor himself."

"Is Holland a first name or last name?" Harli asked.

"Last," Frand said. "Daniel Holland. I'm serious, Harli. He's rotten to the core."

"We have to do something," Harli said. "We have to end this. It's gotten really bad."

"Send me what you have," Frank said. "I'll review it and see if there is anything we can use. We need hard evidence, so send me all of it. Even if you don't think it matters. With any luck, we can move forward with an arrest very soon."

"Okay, Frank," Harli said. "I will."

"I'll talk to you after I review what you give me. And, in the meantime, please stay safe," Frank pleaded.

"We will," promised Harli. "Thanks, Frank." Harli ended the call and stood for a moment in stunned silence. "This is worse than I thought," she whispered into the air. "I need to tell Sebastian."

CHAPTER THIRTY

Once Harli sent the information the group had gathered, she waited for Frank to look it over and call her back. Waiting was difficult, as she wanted answers now, but she knew it would take Frank some time to review the documents. She decided to find Sanchez and fill him in.

After she relayed everything that Frank had told her, Sanchez's eyes were wide open. "I knew he could be dangerous," Sanchez said, "but I was not aware of all this. Frank is right. We need to proceed carefully. Ideally, the FBI will arrest McGreggor on the same night as the escape."

"I agree," said Harli. "But can we coordinate something that large?"

"I'm sure that if we work with the FBI we can make it happen," Sanchez said. "Let's talk to Frank about it when he calls."

"Frank mentioned drugs being shipped from a sugar factory," Harli said. "Should we get another warrant to search the place? They've got to be hiding drugs in that building."

"That explains why McGreggor is so protective of that building," Sanchez acknowledged. "Yes, I am close with a judge who can issue a warrant. I can't call till tomorrow though."

"So, tonight, we wait," Harli sighed.

"I'm afraid so," Sanchez said. "Let's go rejoin the group. I haven't had dessert yet!"

Early the next morning, Harli awoke to her cell phone ringing. She glanced at the caller ID and sat straight up in bed. She clicked the green button, "Frank," she said. "Thanks for getting back to me so quickly. What did you find out?"

"Well, with the original deed to the land, the forged signature, and Andre's payroll records, we have enough for a search warrant," Frank said. "We are going to contact our associates in Honduras, and they are raiding the sugar factory."

Harli jumped up and down. "That's fantastic!" she screamed. The other women in the hut glared at her from their beds. She lowered her voice. "I was going to try to get Sanchez to get a warrant, but it's much more weighted coming from the FBI. Can Sanchez and I tag along?"

"Are you sure?" Frank asked. "It might get messy."

"We've searched there once, looking for Juan Carlos's missing truck, but didn't see anything," Harli offered. "I bet there is a secret room! This is just like a movie."

"Just be careful," Frank warned again. "You're not in a movie; this is real life. With real guns, real bad men, and real danger."

"I understand," Harli said. "Oh, and did you tell your men that a lot of the police and court clerks here are being paid off by McGreggor?"

"Yes, my men know that there are only a few that can be trusted," Frank said. "They are going to the clerk's office to get a blueprint of the building."

"We know someone we can trust at the courthouse," Harli said. "His name is Manuel Escobar."

"Thank you," said Frank. "I'll pass that name along."

"One more thing," Harli said. "When will you serve the warrant?"

"Late tonight," answered Frank. "I'll have my contact call you."

Harli strained to keep the excitement out of her voice. "Okay, Frank. Thanks." She hung up the phone.

"What's that all about?" asked Jexi.

"The FBI is serving a warrant on the sugar factory tonight!" Harli squealed. "This is the biggest case I've ever been involved in!" She opened her contact app and located Sanchez in her favorites. She hit the call button and waited as it rang.

"Hello?" Sanchez said groggily.

"Wake up, sleepyhead!" Harli quipped. "I have news!"

"It's six o'clock in the morning, Harli," Sanchez complained. "Couldn't it wait a few hours?"

"No, it really can't!" Harli said. "Frank told me that the FBI is serving a warrant on the sugar factory tonight. His contact here in Honduras is going to call me so we can accompany them. This is going to get us some answers, Sanchez!"

"That is good news," Sanchez said. "Call me when you hear from them. I'll meet you there. Right now, though, I'm going back to sleep. Oh, and I have an appointment to pick up the explosives later today." He disconnected the call.

Harli stared at her phone in disbelief. Sanchez had hung up on her. She was too excited to go back to sleep, however. She jumped up and got dressed. Then she ran to the center of the village to see if she could help with cooking breakfast. She had to keep herself busy until later that night.

At eight o'clock that evening, Harli's phone rang again. She heard a voice she didn't recognize. "The warrant will be executed at twenty-two hundred hours. Frank said you'd be there. Either make sure you can help or stay out of our way."

Harli scoffed. "Thanks. We'll be sure to be of assistance."

"Affirmative," the man said and then the call ended.

Harli called Sanchez. "It's going down at ten o'clock. Meet me there."

Police cars of all kinds converged upon and surrounded the sugar factory at the designated time. The few guards that were working there were required to put their hands up and the FBI agents removed their weapons and communication devices. The agents entered the building and cleared each room, one by one. They had not found any employees yet, although the parking lot had several cars.

One agent stopped after the rooms had been cleared and demanded to look at the blueprints of the building. He surveyed the form with a puzzled look. "There's a room missing," he bellowed.

Harli recognized the voice as the man who called her earlier to let her know what time to be there. She approached him. "Do you mind if I take a look? Perhaps there is a hidden room," she suggested. She pointed at the blueprints. "See, there is a room outlined right here." She then pointed to a wall. "According to this, the room should be here. But there is a wall that isn't noted on the blueprints."

"Good eye, Detective," the man said.

"I'm a private eye," Harli replied. "But thank you. I've watched a lot of crime dramas. My name is Harli Chase. And you are?"

"Agent Curtis," the man replied. He turned to some other agents. "Find me the entrance to that room." Several men scurried off.

Several minutes later, they heard a shout. "Found it!" someone yelled. Unfortunately, no one could open the door. Agents tried pushing on it, tried to find a switch, and tried knocking it down to no avail.

"How are we going to get in there?" Harli asked Sanchez.

Sanchez looked around. He noticed a fuse box in the corner of the room and decided to check it out. "Come with me," he told Harli. "Everyone get your flashlights and weapons ready," he yelled. "I'm going to try something."

They opened the fuse box and flipped every switch until one last one remained. It was pitch black and everyone had flashlights out. Sanchez hesitated. Harli nudged him. "Go on," she urged. "Flip it."

Sanchez took a breath and flipped the switch. A lock clicked and a beam of light shone from the inside of the secret room. Several men inside the room looked up with surprised faces. The FBI agents rushed in and ordered everyone to lie down on the floor. Inside were tables full of a white powdery substance and all of the machinery needed to create, package, and ship cocaine. All of it was confiscated as Agent Curtis quizzed the men to find out who was in charge.

Finally, one man spoke. "It is Mr. Holland," he said shakily. "Mr. Holland." He pointed in the direction of another man.

Agent Curtis ordered Holland to stand while the others were taken out and processed. "Mr. Holland," he began, "you will be in jail for a very long time with everything we have found here."

"Not likely," Holland answered with a smirk. "I'll be out in no time. But go ahead and dream your little fantasy."

"Take him away," ordered Agent Curtis. Several agents carted him off to a police car.

Sanchez looked at Harli. "Nice work!" he said. "One down and one to go. Maybe you could think about working for me here in Honduras. We work well together, and I'd love to see you every day."

Harli wrung her hands. "Thanks, but I don't think I could leave the States to move to Honduras," she said. "We make a great team, but I have family back home."

As the agents cleaned up the scene, Agent Curtis approached Harli and Sanchez. "Thanks for your help tonight," he said. "Frank told me you were good, but I wasn't sure till I saw you in action. If either of you want a place on the squad, look me up. I need to call Frank and let him know he can move forward with arresting McGreggor. We have enough to put him away."

The two nodded. "Thank you, Agent," said Sanchez.

"I need to call the village," said Harli. "They are going to be thrilled."

CHAPTER THIRTY-ONE

On the evening of the escape attempt, Jexi suddenly became aware of her nerves. Up until that point, she had not been concerned about the plan but now she felt fear for the people involved, especially Hunter. She found him located in the schoolhouse.

"Hunter," she started. "I don't think you should go tonight. There is too much at stake and I don't want you to get hurt."

"Jexi," Hunter replied. "I appreciate your concern, I really do. But it's going to be okay. Besides, all I'm doing is driving the guys to the location. I won't even get out of the car."

"I don't know," Jexi said. "I just got really nervous all of a sudden. I'm scared. How can you be so calm?"

Hunter pulled her into a hug. "I trust God to help us tonight," he said. "The Bible tells us to trust in the Lord with all our hearts and to not lean on our own understanding. I have to believe He is going to protect us from harm."

Jexi relaxed a little. It felt nice having Hunter's arms around her. She didn't want to let go, but she knew Hunter was right. "I know," she said softly. "I believe and trust in Him too. I'm still human though."

Hunter pulled back and smiled. "Your job is to pray tonight. Pray for all of us involved. God will give you the peace your heart needs. And when it's all over, I will give you the biggest hug in the world."

Jexi looked at him and was lost in his eyes for a moment. "Oh, I just remembered," she said. "Ricky and Barrialina want us all to meet at the schoolhouse for prayer before you all leave on your mission."

"I think that is an excellent idea," Hunter said. "But first, we get to eat. I don't know about you, but going back to American food is going to be difficult after having the food here!"

Jexi chuckled. "How can you think about eating at a time like this?" she asked.

Hunter's stomach growled loudly. "That's how!" he said as they both burst laughing.

After dinner, everyone gathered in the schoolhouse for prayer before the mission. Ricky quieted the group and began to pray. "Holy Father God, we give You thanks. We are humbled by how much You love us. We know that we do not deserve Your mercy, but You shower us with it daily. Thank You for all the guidance and protection You have given us so far. Please protect these individuals that are going to rescue Juan Carlos. Place a hedge of protection around them all, including Juan Carlos. Send Your warrior angels to surround them and keep them safe. Please allow the operation to go smoothly with no snags. Thank You for giving us Andre to help. In Jesus' mighty and powerful name, AMEN."

A chorus of *"amens"* erupted from the crowd. Hugs were exchanged and the first leg of the plan was set in motion. Hunter drove the car with Ben in the passenger seat and JC and Antonio in the back. The explosives were in the trunk, rigged with timers and ready to go. They pulled up to McGreggor's property. JC and Antonio got out of the car. Hunter popped the trunk and then walked around to the back of the car. "Do you remember how Sanchez showed you to set the timers? Do you remember how long to set them for?" he asked them.

"Si," JC answered. "We remember."

"We will be careful, senor," Antonio said.

"Please make sure that you are," Hunter replied and got back into the car. He rolled down the window as the boys walked away. "We will be right here when you get done."

"We should pray for them," Ben said. Hunter nodded. Ben began praying. "Father God, we know we have already asked for protection for all of us, but please watch over JC and Antonio as they set these explosives. Keep them in Your hands and guide them to stay safe. Thank You for Your provisions. In Jesus' precious name, amen."

"Amen," echoed Hunter. "How long do you think it will take them?" he asked.

"Shouldn't take more than twenty minutes, I'm pretty sure," Ben responded.

"I hate waiting," Hunter said. "I want to go help them."

"I hear you," Ben said, "but we can't help them. We don't know the terrain like they do. We'd end up getting lost and making things worse. We have to stay here, just like Sanchez told us to."

Hunter's legs were bouncing nervously. "I know," he conceded. "I just hate waiting."

The guys sat in silence for a while as they listened to the sounds of the night.

"Do you think it's dark enough to cover them?" Ben asked. "Definitely," Hunter said. "Plus, like you said, they know the terrain. They know how to get around in the woods without being seen."

Several more silent minutes ticked by. "How long have they been gone?" Hunter asked.

Ben looked at his watch. "Eighteen," he said. He glanced out the window. "They should be back any time now."

They sat through a few more slow minutes. Suddenly they saw some trees move at the edge of the woods. "Is that them?" Ben asked.

Hunter strained his eyes to see in the dark. "I think so, but I can't tell for sure."

"Start the car, just in case," Ben said. "If it's not them, we may need to get away fast."

Hunter started the car. "But if it's not them and we leave, how will they get back?" he asked.

"We don't have a plan for that," Ben said. "So, let's hope it's them!"

Two young men appeared from the woods and ran toward the car. "It's them!" Hunter said in relief. "Ben, text Sanchez and let him know the explosives are in place and armed."

The boys jumped into the back of the car and Hunter started to drive back to the village.

A short time later, Andre approached the guard at the back of the building. "Hey, Ron, how's it going? Sorry you have to work a double shift. Earl called in sick and nobody else was available."

"All good, boss," Ron said. "I need the extra money. It's still and quiet so far. But what are you doing here tonight? Ain't your shift over?"

Andre grunted. "Holland never showed. I can't leave until he gets here, so I'm stuck. I'm not happy about it either."

Ron nodded. "That does suck, boss. Sorry that you are having to pull a double too."

Andre handed Ron a cup of coffee. "That's why I made some coffee. I figured we both could use a bit of help staying awake tonight. Besides, my wife and kids are visiting the in-laws, so they are not home."

"Thanks, boss," Ron said as he took the cup. "I'm not ever going to turn down caffeine!"

"The guys in front have that area secure, so I'll stand watch with you for a while," Andre said. "That Holland better make it back soon."

"Sure, boss, sure," Ron said. "I'm sure he will. I'll bet he's got a good reason."

Andre watched as Ron began sipping the coffee. He also took some drinks of his as he made small talk. He knew in just a matter of a few minutes Ron would be asleep. He took out his phone and sent Sanchez a message. *"The bird is in the cage."*

Sanchez picked up his phone and read the text from Andre. "It's go time," he told Harli and Jessie. The three got into the van and took off toward McGreggor's property. They parked on the north side and waited quietly for the next step. Sanchez held his phone in front of him so he wouldn't miss the next text.

Andre watched Ron as he began to sway back and forth. He also noticed that Ron was slurring his words. *The sleeping pills must be working,* he thought.

"Boss?" asked Ron. "Um, I don't feel so good."

"Sit down for a few minutes and hopefully the feeling will pass," Andre said. "We can't have another man out of commission since we don't know where Holland is."

Ron sat down on the cold concrete. "My head spinnin' . . ." he garbled.

"Shake it off, man," Andre snapped. "I need you at full alert."

"I'mma gonna try, boss," said Ron. He leaned his head against the building and within a minute was snoring.

Andre leaned down and shook him. "Ron, Ron, you okay, man?" He got no response. He tried one more time to shake him awake but Ron remained motionless. Andre took out his cell phone and texted *"The bird is sleeping"* to Sanchez. Andre picked up the coffee cup and placed it under his own. He slowly walked toward the front of the building to wait for phase three.

"That's our cue," Sanchez whispered. "Jessie, stay here unless we alert you to leave. Ready, Harli?"

Harli nodded. They exited the van and walked toward the dense woods. They located the rope that had been placed there previously and then shut off their flashlights. Sanchez led the way as they held onto the rope to navigate the trees. They reached the clearing and waited until they saw the blaze of fire in the distance.

They didn't have to wait long. They saw the night sky light up as the explosives detonated and set things around them on fire. They heard the shouts of the guards at the front of the house, and they heard Andre shout into the walkie-talkie, "Fire! Fire! All hands on deck! Ron, you stay there. We need that entrance guarded. The rest of you come to help! We've got to extinguish those fires before they become widespread and reach the house!" Andre waited until he saw the night man who had been guarding Juan Carlos. He sent another text to Sanchez, *"The cage is empty."*

"Here we go," Sanchez said to Harli. They ran to the back of the house where the tunnel entrance was located. They rushed inside past the sleeping guard and found Juan Carlos in a makeshift cell. "Hurry, Harli, find the keys," Sanchez said. "We don't have a lot of time."

"I know, I know," Harli said as she searched. "They're supposed to be here on the wall. But I can't . . . oh wait! Here they are. They dropped off the hook. Got 'em!" She rushed to the cell and unlocked the door.

Juan Carlos hugged her. "Gracias, senorita, gracias," he said.

"There will be time for hugs later," Sanchez snapped. "Right now, we need to move! We don't know if that guard will wake up soon or not!"

Before she left, Harli snapped several pictures of the basement with her phone. She wanted to have more evidence for Frank.

The three ran through the tunnel and stopped at the open entrance. Sanchez looked around the south side of the property. "Clear," he said. "Make a beeline for the trees. You'll see a rope on the ground."

While they ran for the woods, they could hear the yells of the guards trying to put out the fires. They all grabbed the rope and began their trip to the van. As they went, Sanchez pulled up the rope behind him. He wasn't about to leave any evidence.

They tentatively made their way back to the van and Jessie had the doors open for them. "Get in, get in," she urged. "Quickly!"

They piled in the van, Jessie jumped into the driver's seat and drove away. They all breathed a sigh of relief as they made their way to Choluteca.

Juan Carlos sniffled. "May I have a tissue, please?" he asked. "And a drink of water? It's good to see you again, Miss Jessie."

Harli handed him a tissue and a bottle of water. He took them from her, and she smiled. "My name is Harli Chase," she said. "I am a private detective, and I am so glad to finally meet you!"

Sanchez stuck out his hand. "I am Detective Sebastian Sanchez," he said. "I've also been helping to rescue you."

Juan Carlos wiped his eyes. "I cannot tell you how grateful I am," he said. "I knew my *Dios* would set me free. Thank you all for helping."

Jessie called from the front of the van. "It's good to see you too, Juan Carlos. We have missed you! I am glad you're safe."

"And Angelica?" Juan Carlos inquired. "Will she be at the village?"

"She's safe," Jessie said, "but you're not going back to the village just yet. It's not safe until they get McGreggor arrested. We will take you to a hotel in Choluteca. You'll be safe there until it's all over."

CHAPTER THIRTY-TWO

Andre and his men finally put the fires out around three o'clock in the morning. They were all exhausted, but their shifts weren't over yet. Andre had tried to call Holland, but there had been no response. The guards returned to their stations and then there was a loud shout from the basement.

One of the men frantically ran up the stairs. "He's gone!" he yelled as he ran up to Andre. "The prisoner is gone!"

"What are you talking about?" Andre asked. "He can't be gone."

"He is gone!" yelled the guard. "I swear!"

Andre pushed past the guard and ran down the stairs. He saw the open door where Juan Carlos had been held and pretended to be very angry. How could he have escaped? He couldn't have gone out the front, we would have seen him. And the tunnel, where Ron was covering, is the only other way out! "This is unacceptable!" he bellowed. "I told Ron to stay put!"

Another guard spoke up. "We were busy putting out the fires, boss. Maybe he did get out the front," he suggested.

"Impossible!" Andre yelled. "I made sure to keep an eye on the door for that very reason. Besides, the keys were across the room hanging on that hook." He pointed toward the empty key hook on the wall. "He could not have reached the keys to do this on his own. Where's Ron?"

"You don't think Ron let him out, do you, boss?" asked a guard.

"For his sake, he better not have," Andre said. "McGreggor is not going to like this!" He turned to one of the guards. "Phillips, try to call Holland again. I'm going to look for Ron." He gestured toward the other guard. "Randall, you come with me."

Andre and Randall walked through the tunnel toward the exit. When they walked outside, they found Ron sitting against the house holding his head in his hands.

"Ron!" Andre snapped. "What are you doing on the ground? Get up!" he demanded. "Where is the prisoner?"

Ron's head snapped up in surprise. "I . . . I . . . I don't know what . . . what is happening? My head hurts."

"What do you mean?" Andre asked. "Didn't you hear what was going on through the walkie? It's starting to look like those fires were a diversion to get the prisoner out! You're out here resting, and Juan Carlos is missing!"

"Fires?" Ron asked. "I . . . I really don't know . . ." Ron felt around his head for blood or a knot. "Did someone knock me out?"

Andre scoffed. "You have to be joking. You mean to tell me you've been asleep?"

"I wasn't asleep . . . or was I? I swear I have no idea," Ron replied. "The last thing I remember was talking to you and drinking my coffee."

"The coffee was supposed to keep you awake, not put you to sleep!" Andre yelled. "Now our man's gone, and we will all be on the chopping block! Did you see anything?"

"No, boss," Ron said. "I didn't. I don't remember anything after the coffee. I must have been tired?"

"Stay here," Andre ordered. "And stay awake! Randall, you and Phillips search the area. He might be in the woods nearby. I suspect that those village folk are behind this. I'm going out there to figure this out. Hopefully, we can get the guy back before McGreggor finds out."

"One of us can go with you for backup," said Randall.

"Thanks, but I need you to look for this guy," said Andre. "We really need him back as soon as we can. I can handle these people." Andre jumped into his truck and sped away toward the village.

JC was on watch when he heard the tires of a vehicle pulling into the village and ran to wake the men. "I hear a truck!" he yelled.

Ben and Hunter hadn't been asleep and quickly jumped up to follow JC. "Do you know who it is?" Ben asked.

JC shook his head. "No, I do not recognize the sound of the car."

The truck stopped in front of the schoolhouse and a man exited. Ben, Hunter, and JC stood at the ready, prepared for confrontation. They did not know the man walking toward them.

Andre raised his hands in the air as a gesture of peace. "I am a friend," he said. "Sanchez and Harli told me to come to you and say, *'The bird is out of the cage.'"*

JC pumped his fist in the air. "Papa is free!"

"Praise God!" Ben yelled. He stretched out his hand toward Andre. "Ben Thatcher," he said. "You must be Andre." Andre nodded.

Shaya and Jexi heard the yelling and ran out of their hut. "What's going on?" Jexi asked.

"Sorry," Hunter said. "We didn't mean to wake you."

Shaya shrugged her shoulders. "We weren't asleep," she said. "So, what is going on?"

Ben ran over and hugged her. "Juan Carlos is free!" he said excitedly.

Everyone began to cheer, and the other villagers slowly awakened and joined the group to learn the news. Introductions to Andre were made and an impromptu celebration began.

Angelica emerged from the crowd. "You are the man who helped free my Juan Carlos?" she asked Andre.

"Si," he said. "Juan Carlos is a good man. He deserves to be with his family. I was wrong to help keep him a prisoner. I am so sorry."

Angelica wrapped her arms around Andre's neck as best as she could and squeezed. "Gracias, senor," she whispered as she cried. "Gracias."

"De nada," Andre replied as Angelica pulled away. "But you should thank your husband. He showed me the way to God and for that I will be eternally grateful."

"Oh, my Juan Carlos," Angelica gushed. "He loves the Lord so."

Andre laughed. *"Si!* Very much."

Ben stepped to the front of the crowd and gathered everyone's attention. "People, we indeed have a lot to celebrate and so much to thank God for. But we need to quiet down for now since there are still men patrolling the area for McGreggor. I promise you, we will have a very large celebration as soon as Juan Carlos returns and we are all safe again! But, right now, let us pray and then return to our homes. Please join me.

"Father God, there are not enough words to express our gratitude for everything You have done for us. Thank You for setting Juan Carlos free and keeping him safe. Thank You for this man, Andre, who has helped us. We know in all things that Your will prevails over everything. Please help us finish the plan and protect us all in the process. Thank You, Lord. In Jesus' name, AMEN!"

Andre said a quick goodbye to everyone and got back into his truck. He had a feeling of peace like he had never felt before. He knew that when McGreggor found out about the escape, he could be in grave danger, but he honestly didn't care. He knew he had made the right decision and he finally realized that God would take care of him. He pulled back into McGreggor's driveway. The guards were all waiting for him. As he approached, he remembered to put on his angry face. "Did you have any luck finding the prisoner?" he asked them sternly.

"No, boss," said Phillips. "He's not anywhere around here. He wasn't back at the village?"

"No," Andre said gruffly. "Those villagers had no idea of what I was talking about. They were all sleeping when I got there, so that was a dead end. I even searched the premises."

"Where do you think he could be?" Randall asked.

"Maybe the good Lord took him home," Andre said. "It's like he just disappeared without a trace."

The guys laughed. "But that would mean we were left behind, boss," said Phillips. "I don't like that idea either."

"We'll keep looking," Andre said. "But there's nothing we can do tonight. We can start again tomorrow when there's more daylight. Did anyone get in touch with Holland?"

"No luck," said Randall.

"Something must be wrong," said Andre. "He always answers." He chuckled. "Maybe he got taken, too."

"Ha! Good one, boss!" said Phillips.

"I'm going home to get a few hours of shut-eye before I have to be back here in the morning," said Andre. "Stay vigilant. Call me if anything changes. And make sure Ron stays awake!"

As Andre drove his truck toward home, he couldn't help but smile. He was proud of his performance with the guys. *I should be an actor*; he thought with a chuckle.

When he got to his house, he called Sanchez. "Hola," he said when Sanchez answered. "Everything is covered over here." "Good," Sanchez said. "We just got Juan Carlos settled, and we are headed back. We will contact you in the morning. Harli took pictures of the area where they were holding him captive and sent those to her FBI contact. McGreggor should be arrested by tomorrow night. We have Holland in custody."

"Ah," responded Andre. "That explains a lot. We have been trying to reach Holland for hours."

Sanchez laughed and replied, "I don't think he will be available for a long while!"

CHAPTER THIRTY-THREE

Early the next morning, Harli called Frank. "Hi," she said. "I just wanted to make sure that you got the pictures I sent you."

"I did," Frank said. "But what is that place?"

"That's where they were holding Juan Carlos against his will," Harli answered. "It is in the basement of McGreggor's house in Honduras. We snuck in last night and helped Juan Carlos escape."

"That's bold," Frank commented. "In his own house. Hmm. Well, we have more than enough to arrest him, and I am sure the charges will stick. With what my men have found here in the States and with what you sent us, he will be going away for a long time."

"That's great, Frank!" Harli said. "Will you keep me updated as the case moves forward? There are still a few lackeys here in Honduras to arrest, but we are mainly waiting until McGreggor is behind bars to bring Juan Carlos home."

"Of course," Frank replied. "Thank you for your help, Harli."

"Anytime," she said. "Talk to you soon."

The group was around the picnic tables eating breakfast when Harli found them. She sat down at the table and shared the great news with them. "Sanchez will arrest the few remaining guys working for McGreggor and all we have to do is wait to hear from Frank."

"That's incredible, Harli," Jessie said. "Thank you. What can we do while we wait? Sitting around doing nothing seems pointless. We should do something fun while we have some downtime."

"What about the beach?" Shaya asked.

"I've been thinking the same thing, Shaya," said Hunter.

"Great idea!" said Jessie. "Let's do it!"

Everyone went to their huts to pack and change into their bathing suits.

"This is the first time I've gotten to wear my new honeymoon swimsuit!" Shaya excitedly called from behind the changing curtain. "I hope Ben likes it!"

"He would love whatever you wear," Jexi said giggling. "Even a potato sack!"

Once everyone was ready, they met at the center of the village to pile into the van and Jessie drove them to the beach at Cedeno. They found beach umbrellas and gathered chairs for everyone to sit on. Immediately Jexi headed for the water with Hunter right behind her.

"This reminds me of Aruba!" he said as they eased into the ocean.

"But this time it's much, much better," Jexi said.

"Why is that?" Hunter asked.

"Because now I don't have to pretend that I don't like you," Jexi admitted.

"I knew it!" Hunter said, laughing and pulling her into a hug.

"Yeah, yeah, don't make it weird," Jexi replied. She splashed water on him and attempted to run away. Hunter splashed her back and they fell down in the water.

Ben and Shaya sat in side-by-side chairs and held hands. Shaya chuckled at her friend. "I'm sure glad she's happy," she said. "I worried about her for a while."

Ben smiled. "She just needed some time," he said. "She had a heartbreaking experience, and it was important for God to heal that before she could open herself up to new opportunities."

Shaya squeezed Ben's hand. "You are so wise. How did I get so lucky?"

"We don't believe in luck, remember?" Ben responded.

"You're right," she agreed. "I am so blessed."

Ben sighed. "As much as I miss home, it is going to be very hard to leave this place," he said. "It's so beautiful. And these people are amazing. They are happy in all circumstances, and they don't require all the material things we think we need. It makes our life back home seem so extravagant. I mean, we have so much, it's almost embarrassing. Maybe we can do something about that when we get back." Shaya smiled. "I love that idea!" she agreed. "There is so much we can do to help others. We will get right on that as soon as we get there."

"For now," Ben said, "I'm going to enjoy this beautiful day with my gorgeous wife."

"Wife. I almost forgot we were married," Shaya said. "We've been living in separate huts since we got here."

"I know it's been difficult," Ben said. "But it's been worth it. We have the rest of our lives together."

Shaya stared at the ocean waves lapping the beach. "I admire Angelica and her faith," she said. "I don't know that I could stay so calm if something like that happened to you."

Ben nodded. "I understand, but you are strong in your faith too. Let's just pray that we never have to find out."

The rest of the day was almost as if it was plucked right out of a dream. Between playing in the water and soaking up the sun, the group talked and laughed and made memories. It was late afternoon when Harli's phone rang. Everyone froze in place while she answered the call and placed it on speaker. "Frank, what's the news?" Harli asked.

"We got him," Frank said. The group cheered loudly and danced around on the beach. Frank went on. "He is in custody as we speak. He didn't put up a fight, but he seems to think that he'll be out within the hour. He sure is arrogant."

"Is that possible?" Harli asked. "Can he get out that easily?"

"No," Frank said. "He doesn't know that we specifically found a judge that he doesn't have in his pocket. That judge signed the arrest warrant and will preside at the arraignment. I doubt that he'll be granted bail."

"That is fantastic news!" Harli squealed.

"From what I understand, your boy Sanchez has McGreggor's employees singing like a choir," Frank added.

Harli smiled. "Sanchez is good at his job," she said. "I knew he could do it." Shaya shoved Harli in the shoulder and Harli blushed. Harli waved her off and continued to talk to Frank. "Do you think it's safe for us to bring Juan Carlos home?"

Everyone hovered in silence as they anticipated Frank's response. Finally, they heard, "Yes, bring him home."

"Thank you, Frank," Harli said. "We couldn't have done this without you."

"Likewise, Harli," Frank answered. "You contributed to this case as much as anyone. I meant what I said about that job offer."

"I'll think about it and let you know," Harli said. "Right now, I have a friend to bring home." She hung up the phone and looked at the group. "Let's go get Juan Carlos."

Everyone cheered again. They quickly gathered their belongings and jumped in the van. The perfect day was about to get even better.

"Are you okay?" Hunter asked Jexi as he wiped a tear from her cheek.

"I'm great!" she replied and reached for his hand. "I am so happy for Juan Carlos and his family."

"Me too," Hunter said.

Shaya also wiped tears from her eyes. "Angelica and the kids will be so happy!"

Jessie whooped. "Yes, they will!" she said. "Hey, I'm driving, so one of y'all pray!"

"I will," said Hunter. Everyone except Jessie bowed their heads and closed their eyes. "Oh Father, You have blessed us! You have kept your promise and delivered us from evil. We thank You for the arrest of McGreggor and praise You for the freedom of Juan Carlos and Andre's family. We know that You have heard our prayers and that You have answered us. Lord, bless Andre greatly for what he has done. In the precious name of Jesus, amen."

"Speaking of Andre," Harli said. "I need to call him and let him know his family can come home."

"Hey," said Jexi. "Maybe he can ride in the van when we pick up Juan Carlos, Delfini, and the kids."

"Great idea!" said Harli as her phone rang. She touched the answer button and heard Sanchez's voice.

"Did you hear?" he practically shouted into the phone.

Harli pulled the phone away from her ear. "Yikes! Too loud!" she said. "And yes, we did hear." She put the phone back up. "Frank called. I was just about to call Andre to tell him the news. Jexi suggested that he ride to pick up his family."

"Good idea," Sanchez said. "Sorry for yelling, I am just very excited. I've never been involved in anything so big in my career. It's a huge thing for me! But I have already called Andre. I can call him back and let him know that the van will pick him up. Who is driving up?"

"We hadn't decided," Harli said, "but JC will probably want to."

"Okay, I'll pass along the message," Sanchez said. His tone softened. "Hey, Harli, I just wanted to say, great work. I guess you'll be going home soon."

"Yeah, probably," Harli said. "I mean, now that McGreggor has been taken in, the case is closed."

Sanchez was silent for a moment. "Would you like to have dinner with me before you leave?" he asked shyly.

It was Harli's turn to be silent. "Um, well, yeah," she said. "I think I would."

Sanchez smiled and was secretly glad she couldn't see his face. "Great!" he said. "I'll set something up for tomorrow night."

"Good plan," Harli said. "But you can also come out to the village tonight if you'd like to see Juan Carlos's homecoming. We are planning a big party."

"Oh, really?" Sanchez asked. "I can?"

"Well, sure," Harli answered. "You were pretty instrumental in solving this thing. I think it would be great to have you there."

Sanchez was glad once again that she couldn't see his face as he blushed. "I'll be there," he said. "Thanks."

Harli clicked the end call button and looked up to see Jexi and Shaya's faces with huge smiles just staring at her. "What?" she asked.

"Just admit it," Shaya said. "You've got a thing for him."

"Fine, maybe a little," Harli admitted. "But it would never work. I'm going back to the States, and he lives here. Besides, I don't even think he looks at me as more than a colleague."

Hunter patted Jexi's leg and glanced at Harli with sympathy. "Leave the poor girl alone," he said. "You had a secret thing for me once upon a time too."

Jexi rolled her eyes. "You're never going to let me live that down, are you?" she asked.

Hunter laughed. "Nope. Never."

"I'm sorry, Harli," Shaya said. "It's just that the two of you make such a cute couple!"

Jexi chimed in. "I'm sorry too," she said. "We'll leave you alone about it. We just enjoy a good love story."

"Thank you," Harli said. "But there's no love story here."

"Yet," Shaya whispered.

"We heard that," said Ben. "I thought Jexi just said that you two would leave her alone."

"What?" Shaya replied. "I was simply finishing her sentence for her."

Harli laughed nervously, "Can we talk about something else, please? Anything else?"

"We are almost at the village," said Jessie. "Get ready to plan a party!

CHAPTER THIRTY-FOUR

The van pulled back into the village a couple of hours later, as everyone anxiously waited. The door opened and the first one out was Juan Carlos. Angelica ran to him and embraced him, and the children also gathered around him. They all cried while they hugged and kissed each other. Juan Carlos never wanted to let them go.

Andre exited the van next, and the entire village erupted in cheers and applause of gratitude. Andre hung his head. "I do not deserve your kindness," he said to the crowd.

The men of the village approached Juan Carlos and Andre and lifted them up onto their shoulders as the rest of the villagers shouted with glee. They walked the men to the center of the village where the party had been prepared. The sight was amazing, and Juan Carlos cried more because he was finally home. When they had been set down Juan Carlos reached for Andre and pulled him into a hug. "Gracias, amigo," he whispered.

Andre was also crying and all he could muster back was a quiet, *"De nada."*

JC stood up on a table and banged a metal spoon against a pot to silence everyone. When the cheers and clapping had subsided, he addressed the crowd. "People of Aldea Gracia, today is a magnificent day! *Mi* papa is home!" The crowd erupted again. JC shushed everyone. "We have new friends, Andre, Delfini, and their children, Paulo and Elena! Our land is also safe from now on! McGreggor and his associates are in jail! God has delivered us! We are free!"

The crowd went wild. Everyone was so happy and overjoyed that all of these problems had been solved. JC waited for them to return to calm. "But I don't want to forget to say thank you to our American friends and Officer Sanchez," JC added. "Without them, we would not be celebrating today." With that, more cheers and adulation burst forth from the villagers. JC paused and then said, "Okay, one more thing since I have your attention." He turned to Maya, the love of his life. "Maya, can you come up here with me?"

Maya looked stunned but climbed up onto the table next to him and he took her hand. JC lowered his body to one knee and pulled a small box out of his pocket. Everyone gasped. Maya began to cry. "Maya," JC began, "I have loved you for a very long time. I have spoken with your father, and he has given me his blessing to ask for your hand in marriage. I do not want to spend another day without you. Would you please marry me?"

The people waited almost silently as they anticipated her answer. Maya looked into JC's eyes as tears fell from hers. She gripped his hands and softly whispered, *"Si, mi amor.* Yes!" JC slipped the ring onto her finger and Juan Carlos bellowed, "My son is getting married! *Dios* keeps pouring out his blessings on us all!" Once again, the people began to applaud.

Jexi sidled up next to Shaya. "This day has been perfect," she told her best friend. "Thank you for coming and for bringing Harli."

Shaya shoved Jexi playfully. "You're making it weird," she said laughing.

Jexi laughed and said, "Yeah, I am, aren't I?"

"It's okay," Shaya said. "I'm glad we came. It's not the honeymoon we planned but I am blessed to be a part of this. It was God's plan for us and I'm just happy we said 'Yes' to His call."

"Now who's making it weird?" Jexi laughed.

"There is nothing weird about doing God's work," Shaya said playfully.

"No, you're right. I didn't mean to sound flippant. I get it," said Jexi. "When we say 'yes' to Him, we are blessed beyond measure. So, speaking of blessings . . . I need to find my BOYFRIEND."

Shaya snickered. "You just love saying that, don't you?" Jexi nodded. Shaya rolled her eyes. "I'm happy for you, you know."

As Jexi briskly walked away, she called over her shoulder, "You're making it weird again!"

After Jexi found Hunter among the crowd, they spent the remainder of the evening with Ben and Shaya. The four marveled at how God had worked over the last several weeks and how full their hearts were right at this moment.

By the time the party was over, and things cleaned up, everyone was exhausted. Throughout the village, the extinguished lanterns were followed by happy dreams.

The next day, Jessie met with Harli, Ben, Shaya, Hunter, and Jexi to discuss the details of returning to the States. "Are you guys ready to head home, or do we need a few more days here?" Jessie asked. "Either way, we need to decide so we can purchase our tickets home."

"Let's wait two more days," suggested Shaya. "That gives us time to help Juan Carlos get settled and time to say goodbye to everyone. It sounds like Andre and Delfini are going to sell their house and move to the village, we can also help clear out a hut for them."

"Plus," Jexi said, "Harli can have her date with Sebastian."

Harli blushed. "Did you have to mention that?" she asked.

Jessie smiled. "When is the big night?" she inquired.

"It's tonight," said Harli, shooting a glare toward Jexi.

"Well, have fun," Jessie said. "He's a nice man. I will start getting our plane tickets. Plan for departure the day after tomorrow."

Hunter took Jexi's hand and looked at Ben and Shaya. "That gives us two days to play around Honduras!" he said excitedly. "Let's find out what there is to do."

"Jexi and I definitely need to do some shopping!" Shaya said.

"Shopping?" Ben asked with an eyebrow raised.

"Only for souvenirs!" Shaya said. "For other people!"

"It's fine, hon," said Ben chuckling. "I'm just teasing. I trust you to not go overboard."

Jexi laughed. "That's right!" she said. "You are married now and have to check with your husband first."

"Not exactly, Jexi," Ben said. "But Shaya was just talking about not wanting to have a lot of material things. I was just sparking her memory. She can buy whatever she wants."

Harli stood to go to the hut. "If you'll excuse me, I need to get ready for tonight," she commented. Her stomach filled with butterflies as she prepared for her date with Sebastian. *Is this a date?* she thought. *I wonder what he is thinking. I hope I'm not reading too much into this.* She gave herself one last glance in the mirror, gathered the keys to the van and began the drive to Choluteca. She had agreed to meet him at a restaurant since it didn't make a lot of sense to have him drive to the village and back to the city.

Once at the restaurant, she parked the van and walked inside. She saw him sitting in a booth waiting for her. He noticed her, stood up, and waved her over. She took a deep breath and exhaled slowly. *Here we go,* she thought. She approached him and he stepped forward and gently kissed her on the cheek. Her stomach fluttered even more. "Hi," she muttered.

"Good evening," Sebastian said. "You look beautiful."

Harli smiled. "Thank you," she said. "You clean up pretty good yourself!"

"I got us a booth," Sebastian said. "I hope that's okay."

"It's great," Harli answered as she sat down opposite him. "This is a nice restaurant. Do you come here a lot?"

Sebastian laughed nervously. "Sometimes," he said. "They have good steaks here."

Harli kicked herself for being so nervous. *You've worked beside him for weeks,* she chastised herself. *You've never been this rattled. It's just Sanchez after all!* "Steak sounds delicious," she said.

They made small talk about the case throughout dinner. When they were done eating, there was an awkward silence between them.

Sebastian cleared his throat and said, "When are you going back to the States?"

"Day after tomorrow," Harli said.

"I bet you'll be happy to be home," Sanchez said.

"Yeah, it will be nice," she responded.

Sanchez reached for Harli's hand. "I will miss you," he said quietly. This time, Harli didn't pull away. His hand felt comfortable and familiar, like she'd known him for as long as she could remember.

"I'm going to miss you, too," she admitted. It was nice to finally get that off her chest. "We really work well together, Sanchez. I've enjoyed working on this case with you."

"Can I call you sometime?" Sanchez asked. "I don't want to stop talking to you. You've become special to me."

"Look, I'll be honest," Harli said. "I like you too. But I'm worried. Long distance relationships are usually doomed from the start."

"I know," Sanchez said. "I understand that I can't really get what I want right now. That doesn't mean we can't be friends who talk, right?"

"We can be friends," Harli said. "I'm sorry it can't be more."

"It's okay," said Sanchez. "I just want you in my life in some way."

Sanchez walked Harli out to her car. "I know we aren't going to be an item," he said. "But can we pretend that we are for just a moment?" He leaned in and kissed her on the lips.

Harli responded to him and returned the kiss. As they pulled away from each other, she smiled. "I enjoyed pretending for that moment," she said. "It's going to be difficult to return to reality. If you'd like, we can pretend some more tomorrow night. There's a going away bonfire at the village and I'm inviting you."

The rest of the evening was comfortable and flirty. Harli wished this didn't have to end. They reluctantly said goodnight with the promise of another evening together.

The big bonfire and dinner were to honor Jessie, Harli, Sebastian, Ben, Shaya, Hunter, and Jexi for all of their help. It was the last night in the village and the group soaked up every ounce of love that was offered to them. Harli and Sebastian held hands practically the entire evening. Hunter and Jexi talked with JC and Maya about their wedding plans. Ben and Shaya played with the small children and Shaya found herself grinning at seeing little Natalia sitting on Ben's lap. Jessie talked with Andre and his family about the upcoming sale of their house. She was excited that they were moving to the village. The night and the entire trip had been a journey none of them would soon forget.

After eating one of the most delicious meals they'd ever had, they roasted marshmallows and shared stories. As the last sliver of sunlight sat on the horizon, Juan Carlos stood to make a speech. "I am humbled at the love God has shown to me," he began. "I do not deserve such wonderful family and friends. I did not know when Jessie introduced me and my family to Jesus, what that would mean for us. God has a will for our lives. That does not mean that we will not face troubles. It was no mistake that I was taken by McGreggor's men, and I am not angry that I endured this. God knew that I would meet a man named Andre who would need Him. I was put there just so I could show Andre the love of God. If I had not been kidnapped, this could not have happened." Juan Carlos looked at Andre and nodded. "I am glad to be submitted to God's will. Because I listened to Him, I was rescued, and more importantly, Andre has joined God's kingdom." Everyone clapped and cheered with joy. When it had quieted, Juan Carlos wrapped up his speech. "I welcome Andre and his family to our community. At the same time, I once again thank our friends for their assistance and wish them safe travels. We will miss you. Pray with me, *por favor. Dios,* we are grateful for our safety and Your blessings. Please keep us all in the center of Your will. Keep our friends safe as they travel. We love You. In Jesus' name, amen." Everyone turned back to the celebration.

"God always amazes me," said Shaya. "But I really shouldn't be amazed! I know that He can do all these things and infinitely more, so I shouldn't be amazed. Yet, every single time, I'm always amazed!"

"I think that's the point," Hunter said. "I believe that He wants us to be amazed each time."

"That way we never lose the wonder at how incredible He is," said Jexi.

"Exactly," said Ben. "And I, for one, never ever want to lose that wonder."

They all leaned back in their chairs to take in the beauty of the night. It was a clear sky, and the stars shined so brightly it appeared as if they could almost touch them. As if on cue, a shooting star blazed across the sky, and the group gasped.

"I love it when He shows off," laughed Jexi.

Shaya put her head on Jexi's shoulder. "He's letting us know He sees us, and we are loved."